MW00945487

Surviving Disaster Without Leaving Home

First Edition

Look for our companion book:

Evacuation: A Family Guide for The 21st Century

(ISBN: 9781461024866)

Also see our website:

World Disaster Report
www.wdrep.com

Acknowledgements: We would like to acknowledge the following friends for their contribution to the content of this book Stan Padgett, Gregg Boyer, Lamar Gourley, George Owen, Stan Edwards, Chris Rusch, for technical input from Stanley Miller, Jessica Marsaw and to the "Editor and Chief": Karen Jones.

Disclaimer: This book is intended to stimulate individual and family review and planning to increase comfort during an emergency and personal basic security. The information and authors' opinions contained herein are not to be considered legal or economic advice. Individuals and families should consider this information and make their own plans based on careful research and adaptation to their own situation. The authors assume no liability of any kind in connection with these opinions. It is certain that some will disagree with the opinions expressed herein. Your actions should be your own after making informed decisions based on the various opinions expressed to you. The opinions we offer should be considered only one of those various opinions.

Surviving Disaster
Without Leaving Home

A disaster, man-made or natural, may create an environment where you find yourself removed from all public services and left to make it through with what you have on hand. There are no police to protect you, no fireman to rescue you. You are cut off from the outside world. The stores are closed or inaccessible; there are no gas stations open for 100 miles. Evacuation may or may not be an option. In any event, you decide to stay where you are and to make do with what you have.

One of the most important decisions you will make is whether or not to "tough it out "and to stay in place during an unrest of nature or man. The best decision is the one that will secure the safety of yourself and your family. If you cannot be sure of your safety, you need to evacuate. Once you make the decision to stay, your options may become very limited very fast. You must have all materials in play.

While this book is not designed as a "survivalist" guide for the long term situation, it will help you through a short term emergency (3-30 days) until normalcy returns. The principles learned could be applied for a longer term situation. By learning how to store and use available resources and to adapt what you have to what you need, you will be prepared for the worst situations.

If you decide to stay, this book will help you prepare to shelter in place. By following the procedures outlined, you can make sheltering-in-place an enjoyable and memorable experience: Imagine that!

HOW TO USE THIS MANUAL

This book is divided into two major sections: ***Things to Consider and Scenarios***. It is intended to help you overcome any challenge while at home and facing an interruption of public services. It is easy to become overwhelmed when addressing problems and to consider how far you have to go to be prepared for them. Therefore, we will give you the tools for overcoming the issues (scenarios) before we address the issues themselves.

- **Things to Consider**:

There are nine major items to consider. Each of these major subjects should be reviewed well in advance if you plan to "weather" a storm (natural or manmade). Security can be an overwhelming issue independent of the others. Because of its scope and reach, it is addressed independently in detail in chapter 20.

You may be tempted to review just the ones that are of particular interest to you. But know that many of the guidelines taught in the individual sections will apply to other scenarios and may not be covered again. For example, medical issues are discussed throughout the text as their particular interests are addressed.

- **Possible Scenarios:**

There are eight possible emergency scenarios reviewed. There are two where staying at home is not an option: flood and wildfire. These two are addressed in the Chapter 19: Evacuation: the Only Option.

A hurricane produces windstorm and flooding. In the *Hurricane* scenario you will be referred to the *Tornado* section for the construction of safe rooms needed in case of windstorm and to the *Flood* section for issues associated with rising water. You will be referred to other relative sections in the book by the symbol:
⇨

Following the scenarios, direction is given on how to carry out your plan. Forms are provided to assist you in determining needed resources to weather the storm. After you have studied the material you will need to get started on creating your own plan and carrying it out. We encourage you to include your family and friends in the planning process.

CONTENTS

9

Chapter 1

GETTING STARTED

Personal emergencies seem to be a remote possibility for most of us. It is always something that happens to the "other guy" and we see it in all of its drama during the cable news broadcast. We watch with interest and concern but later turn the TV off and go in for our evening meal. It is a memory by morning and is the topic of discussion with coworkers the next day.

However; every once in a while, the emergency presents itself at our door step. It can come in many varieties. It may be an event that affects a large area or just us. It could be as simple as a loss of a job or as serious as a national catastrophe. In any case, we need to be prepared.

We spoke to a mom who experienced the Huntsville tornado disaster in April 2011. Her husband was away on business and she was home alone with three small children. Here is a copy of an excerpt from her personal blog following the event:

"....Lastly, you've asked for emergency preparedness tips. Here's what I've compiled for life without power in a natural disaster area:"

"1. Food: Food that requires no preparation, no hot water, no cooking. Warning: granola bars and peanut butter crackers get old really fast. I was frustrated that I had lots of food stored and *no way to cook it.*

2. Food Preparation: Extra propane for the grill, a camp stove with extra propane, a Dutch oven with charcoal. Where would I have set up a dutch oven fire ring? My patio?? Need to think that one through.

3. Food Preservation: Your frig and freezer are gone along with all the food in them. This sucks. Which brings me to…

4. A Generator: This is your life line. It can power your frig or freezer, allow you to charge up phones, laptops, or radios. This one item will make a huge difference. Don't forget to have gas to power it. Which brings me to…

5. Gas: A lot of people would have left our area but for the lack of gas. I had a sparkling 1/4 tank when the storms hit. You can't escape the crisis if you had no gas. And in our area, there wasn't gas for 100 miles in any direction. Beware though, gas doesn't store well and has to be rotated regularly. But trust me; you'll be glad you have it.

6. Cash: "Cash only" became the policy around here. Have some in the house for when you need it.

7. Battery operated radio: This became the most useful thing any of us had. This was our entire communication system for the north half of the state. This was how we got updates on the storm damage, what the local and national government were working on, the situation with the power plant, where to find ice, where a lone gas station might be open, and what time of day it was… Radio was everything.

8. Battery operated clock: This may seem silly but if there is no electricity, you won't know what the time is.

9. Phone with a cord: Cordless phones don't work if the power is out. Phone lines came back before the electricity did. Those with a cord could speak. Those without, cursed their lifeless phones. Remember: cell phones don't work. Towers are swamped; people could not get calls in or out. This was lousy.

10. Gas water heater: Ha! I had one. This meant – hot showers. Everyone with an electric heat pump in their house went for days without bathing. Gross. If yours is electric, find a friend with a gas one or you goin' be diiiirty.

11. Light sources: It gets very, very dark at night. Very. Freaks the kids out. Freaks me out. Have working flashlights, have lots of candles. Have glow sticks or an equivalent to leave in your kids' rooms as a night light. My kids couldn't sleep in the dark. A friends' loaned reading lamp saved us all.

11

12. Paper products and plastic bags: Power goes out you have no dishwasher. Washing all dishes by hand gets old fast. Have a bunch of paper plates, cups, and plastic utensils. Also, plastic bags have many grand uses. Imagine me warming up a can of corn dumped in a plastic bag and drowned in a bowl of hot water. Sounds delicious, right?

13. Clean clothes: Power goes out and you have no clean laundry. Imagine washing clothes by hand. No, don't. If you've got an extra change of clothes in your 72 hour kits you know you'll always have at least one clean outfit.

14. A bike: Imagine life with no gas for your car. You'll be glad to have a man powered vehicle.

15. Gun: Sad but true. People panicked quickly and looters started looking for an easy pick. They hit the storm damaged areas within hours of the tornadoes looking for anything and everything. We had a group of looters canvassing our neighborhood by night #2. And I live in a nice neighborhood! In a nice town! Incredible. A little "che che" sound of a loaded shotgun might have changed their minds. And for some of the families that left town, the husbands and dads stayed behind to protect the homestead. True story.

Lastly, both husband and wife need to know the plan. Together (my husband) and I are prepared, by myself? I get a D+. I've decided to learn how to cook in the wild. Good thing I already know how to shoot straight."

Here are a few examples of other events which have occurred recently that may give reason for concern,

EXAMPLES OF EVENTS TO PREPARE FOR:

- **EARTHQUAKE:** August 23, 2011 Rocked the East coast causing the North Anna power station in Spotsylvania, County, Va. to shutdown.
- **WINTER STORMS:** Winter 2011 Devastated the Midwest with massive amounts of snow and sustained cold. For the first time in decades, it snowed on Christmas day in Atlanta, Gerogia.
- **VOLCANO:** June 2011: Volcano erupts in Puyehue Chili devastating parts of Argentina with ash and creating spectacular electrical storms.
- **TORNADO:** May 2011: An unprecedented outbreak in tornado activity across the Midwest and the south east United States. The largest death toll from a single tornado in history in Joplin, Missouri.

- o April 2011: A mile wide tornado from the deadly April 25 outbreak struck Tuscaloosa and Birmingham, Alabama. At least one tornado also struck Huntsville Alabama destroying the electric grid for many miles and damaging the Brown's Ferry Nuclear Power Station. The Nuclear plant was shut down as a precautionary measure. Motor fuel and other supplies were unavailable for fifty or more miles and electric power for most of the city was out. Hundreds of thousands of households were affected even though they were not hit directly by the storm. The Mayor of Huntsville recommended the entire city to evacuate if they were able.
- **EARTHQUAKE AND TSUNAMI:** March 11, 2011: devastated coastal Japan. Deaths number in tens of thousands, and homeless exceed several hundred thousand. Nuclear reactor safety systems failed in the aftermath of tsunami destruction. Infrastructure was devastated over a wide area making rescue and relief impossible for an extended period.
- **NUCLEAR POWER PLANT: -** If the THREE MILE ISLAND plant (or other nuclear plant) today experienced a catastrophic meltdown and containment vessel rupture, people who live within about a 20 mile region of the plant (who are exposed to the radioactive plume) may be subject to the dangers of acute radiation poisoning (with symptoms appearing relatively rapidly) as well as long-term health effects like thyroid cancer. If people are not adequately sheltered or evacuated in a timely fashion from this region and are exposed to high levels of radiation, they could experience severe sickness and possible death within a few days to months. (as subsequently reported by FEMA)
- **GULF OF MEXICO OIL CATASTROPHE**: June 25, 2010 (Examiner.com) "As FEMA and other government agencies prepare for what is now being called the worst oil spill disaster in history, plans to evacuate the Tampa Bay area are in place. The plans would be announced in the event of a controlled burn of surface oil in the Gulf of Mexico, or if wind or other conditions are expected to take toxic fumes through Tampa Bay." (this eventuality was never carried out, but was seriously considered)
- **WILDFIRE:** September 2011: The most destructive single fire on record swept across parts of Texas destroying 32,330 acres near Houston and 52,951 near the Louisiana border killing two people. It was not until cooler temperatures and the weekend rains came that firefighters were able to get a handle on it.

- **A MASSIVE EARTHQUAKE:** May 12, 2008, struck the eastern Sichuan Province of central China near Chengdu, on Monday afternoon (local time). The quake killed thousands, and injured thousands more who were trapped under the rubble of collapsed buildings.
- **FLOODS:** October 2009: ATLANTA GEORGIA residents had about thirty minutes to leave before flood waters entered their homes. The MIDWEST experienced massive flooding from the Mississippi river.
    - **September 2011:** Hurricane Irene caused unprecedented flooding in the New England states of the eastern seaboard. Catastrophic property damage was experienced as well as loss of life.
- **HURRICANE:** August 28, 2005, Hurricane Katrina was in the GULF OF MEXICO where it powered up to a Category 5 storm on the Saffir-Simpson hurricane scale packing winds estimated at 175 mph. At 7:10 a.m. EDT on August 29, Hurricane Katrina made landfall in southern Plaquemines Parish Louisiana, just south of Buras, as a Category 3 hurricane. Maximum winds were estimated near 125 mph to the east of the center.
    - Hurricane Andrew, in 1992, cost approximately $21 billion in insured losses (in today's dollars), whereas estimates from the insurance industry as of late August 2006, have reached approximately $60 billion in insured losses (including flood damage) from Katrina. The storm could cost the Gulf Coast states as much as an estimated $125 billion. (NOAA.gov)

When reviewing events such as these, you will find some things in common. Here is what you can expect immediately following an emergency:

UNAVAILABILITY OF SUPPLIES AND SERVICES

The following supplies and services would be affected by a **major regional disaster**. General research suggests that their availability might be affected as noted below. Regional disasters that occur with some prior warning (volcanic activity, hurricanes, and severe weather outbreaks) will create scarcity in varying ways.

Scarce within 24 – 48 hours
- Cell phone service is questionable depending on the event from immediately after the emergency
- Food: (grocery and convenience stores will be mostly stripped)

- Fuel: Both gasoline and diesel stocks will be quickly diminished-some stations may limit purchases to a few gallons. Stocks will not disappear immediately but they cannot be replenished (supply cannot keep pace with demand) until normal routines return.
- Cash: Banks may not be able to open if personnel do not report for work or if electrical power is absent or intermittent. Banks also carry only a limited amount of actual currency and without resupply these stocks might quickly be depleted by high local demand.
- Local business: These would be directly impacted as fuel stocks diminished.
- Raw materials: Wood, various building material components, plastic tarps

Scarce within 48-72 hours
- Medical supplies (both in drug stores and physicians offices).
- Normal physician office services may be interrupted as staff fail to report for work
- Truck transportation: This would suffer quickly due to personnel (driver) absence and fuel scarcity. Since most everything is transported at some stage via truck, unpredictable shortages would develop and hoarding behavior would probably commence as shortages became noticeable.

Scarce within 3-5 days
- **Hospital stocks** may last as much as one week until lack of delivery begins to have major effects. This includes both private physician surgery centers and hospital based surgery, both of which depend heavily on timely delivery of disposable medical supplies and drugs.
- **Electric:** A total failure of a regional power grid would suppose heavy damage to fuel and/or actual transmission infrastructure. Electric providers have mutual aid agreements with surrounding areas and are thus more resilient. However, recovery from a major regional disaster supposes the availability of critical supplies, personnel and fuel to sustain the repair effort.
- **Fire services:** These will diminish unless fuel and personnel are well supported. These services require a minimum number of personnel to staff engines and maintain effective constant coverage.
- **Local/county/state police services**: These might have to be severely scaled back unless fuel stocks could be replenished. A significant number of police may fail to report for duty, making coverage intermittent, if looting or civil disorder begins. They may remain home to be sure their own families are protected.

- **Federal Government (local offices):** Services (various offices and departments) will probably not be fully staffed, thus increasing their usual inefficiency.
- **Postal services:** These are heavily dependent on fuel and personnel in sufficient quantities and normal interstate transportation is necessary for this to be effectively continued.

Scarce greater than 30 days

- **Telephone and regional internet service:** These services are heavily computerized and will likely continue unless specific infrastructure damage occurs. If such conditions exist restoring normal function could require a very long time.

Services that will continue

Local churches: Local communities tend to have cohesion based on common belief, familiarity and intentions. Untold good has been done in the past by such groups even in the face of severe disasters.

Local farmers' markets/yard sales: These may continue in significant volume due to proximity or supplies to consumers.

Some federal government services: The federal government control is hierarchical, highly distributed (having many branch offices across the country), thus will likely continue to be influential in some form for an extended period. Staffing would be expected to suffer as other government offices for the same reasons depending on local circumstances. As the regional problem continues, federal effectiveness would diminish due to staffing, communications and fuel issues.

Tax collections by federal, State and local government: This function would probably continue in some form no matter what other disaster occurred.

National Guard: This force would suffer from no-shows in event of a regional disaster; however if federalized, it might receive support from more distant bases that had sufficient fuel and logistics stocks.

Federal Armed Forces: Army, Navy, Air Force, Marines, Coast Guard and subsidiary units: These are under Federal control and can thus draw personnel and supplies from other areas if necessary. These forces might be regionally isolated due to materiel shortages but command and control would still be exerted (with varying success) from national headquarters.

HAM radio as an information source: This community is often an informal mixture of hobbyists and serious participants. County emergency management agencies employ the use of these operators.

THINGS TO CONSIDER

Chapter 2

FOOD AND WATER

Food Storage becomes a necessity if you intend to shelter in place anywhere. A habit of stocking up on needed items would be a good one to acquire. It must be stored it in a place that would be protected from damage, in the safe room or shelter you will be occupying.

FOOD AND BASIC NECESSITIES

- Organize your food inventory into the following categories immediately if you are going to stay in your home. Each category will be handled differently.
    o Dry staples requiring cooking.
    o Food items not requiring cooking.
    o Refrigeration (residual cold) may last 24 hours if the refrigerator is left completely undisturbed. The freezer items should last three days. You need to consider what you will do if the power outage extends beyond that point. Cooking meats and other frozen items on the backyard grill is one possibility, but then how will you store the cooked items so they will not quickly spoil? Depending on the situation, salting meat may be an option but that is a skill that you must acquire <u>before</u> the emergency occurs. If you keep a large amount of food in your freezer much of it will likely be wasted.
    o Snacks (control these carefully or they will be eaten too quickly).
    o Garden items (if you have a garden)

THREE-MONTH SUPPLY
Build a small supply of food that is part of your normal, daily diet. One way to do this is to purchase a few extra items each week to build a one-week supply of food. Then you can gradually increase your supply until it is sufficient for three months. These items should be rotated regularly to avoid spoilage.

- Make a list of foods you eat every day to determine how much you would use in 1 month and then build up to 3 months.
- Gradually purchase these foods in bulk as they go on sale or buy 1 or 2 extra items each time you shop to build up your supply or buy it all at once. Do whatever works best for you.
- Remember that some items can be in the refrigerator/freezer.
- Use and rotate this food in our daily cooking.
- Replenish the food you have used as it goes on sale again

- Don't forget to store non-food items. Get a 3 month supply of toiletries, medications, diapers, etc.[1]
- Benefits include: saving money by buying food on sale and always having the food you eat on hand.

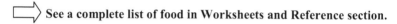 **See a complete list of food in Worksheets and Reference section.**

DRINKING WATER

Store drinking water for circumstances in which the water supply may be polluted or disrupted. If water comes directly from a good, pretreated source, then no additional purification is needed; otherwise, pre-treat water before use. Store water in sturdy, leak-proof, breakage-resistant containers. Consider using plastic bottles commonly used for juices and soda. Keep water containers away from heat sources and direct sunlight. Of course, during extreme emergency, try the nearest fire hydrant. With a large pipe wrench and a "cheater bar" there is a good chance that you may find some there.

FINANCIAL RESERVE

Establish a financial reserve by saving a little money each week and gradually increasing it to a reasonable amount. Have plenty of small bills.

LONGER-TERM SUPPLY

For longer-term needs, and where permitted, gradually build a supply of food that will last a long time and that you can use to stay alive, such as wheat, white rice and beans. These items can last 30 years or more when properly packaged and stored in a cool, dry place. A portion of these items may be rotated in your three-month supply. You may also want to add other items to your longer-term storage such as sugar, nonfat dry milk, salt, baking soda and cooking oil. To meet nutritional needs, also store foods containing Vitamin C and other essential nutrients.

- It would be wise to maintain a significant supply (minimum of six months) of staple food items (beans, rice, pasta etc.) in an easily stored form (cans or Mylar pouches).
- Water is critical to survival but even in a disaster pressure remains for a time in the water lines. Make a plan to fill specific containers for drinking and other uses. You will need to access these containers quickly in the event of impending trouble, so store them accordingly.
- Potable water remains in toilet flush tanks and water heaters. Make a plan as to how you will remove this water and for what purposes you

---

[1]Providentliving.com

will use it. Rationing will be necessary, with primary attention to personal hydration.

The loss of power is an inconvenience with most other "creature comforts; however, the loss of electricity in regards to food can be devastating. In the case where the loss of power may be lengthy, the ability to keep food useable is critical. Therefore it is important to consider options to maintain critical services to the home.

⇨ *(Study the chapter on electrical.)*

Get into the habit of purchasing more food than you need every time you go to the grocery store. Purchase the things that you would normally buy. Buy things that your family likes to eat with the attention to the detail of shelf life. Most food items will have a shelf life printed on the package. Devise a method of rotating the food so that you will have a good supply and keep within the expiration date prior to consumption.

Simple pantry/shelf management may be sufficient; however, you can make this effort very manageable by making or purchasing "rear load" shelving devises. If you always load the shelves from the rear and remove them from the front, they will always be on the shelf an equal amount of time. These works best for canned goods. The image below shows one example: http://beprepared.com/. This is a simple way of keeping everything fresh.

Storage under beds, couches and some tables provide storage in areas not otherwise considered. Some life sustaining foods can be stored in bulk and have a very long shelf life. There are many places on the web that assists in the storage and preservation of bulk food items. Honey, wheat and lintels are some Examples.

WATER STORAGE GUIDELINES

Commercially bottled water in PETE (or PET) plastic containers may be purchased. Follow the container's "best if used by" dates as a rotation guideline. Avoid plastic containers that are not PETE plastic[2].

If you choose to package water yourself, consider the following guidelines:

Containers

- Use only food-grade containers. Smaller containers made of PETE plastic or heavier plastic buckets or drums work well.
- Clean, sanitize, and thoroughly rinse all containers prior to use. A sanitizing solution can be prepared by adding 1 teaspoon (5 ml) of liquid household chlorine bleach (5 to 6% sodium hypochlorite) to one quart (1 liter) of water. Only household bleach without thickeners, scents, or additives should be used.
- Do not use plastic milk jugs, because they do not seal well and tend to become brittle over time.
- Do not use containers previously used to store non-food products.

---

[2] Fema.gov, epa.gov

WATER PURIFICATION GUIDELINES

If your water supply is not known to be safe or has become polluted, it should be purified before use. Water purification is generally a two-step process.[3]

Step 1: Clarify

Cloudy or dirty water must first be made clear. It may be passed through filter paper, fine cloth, or other filter. It may be allowed to settle and the clear water on top carefully drawn. *Filtered or clear settled water should always be disinfected before use.*

Step 2: Disinfect

- ### Boiling Method

Bringing water to a rolling boil for 3 to 5 minutes will kill most water-borne microorganisms. However, prolonged boiling of small quantities of water may concentrate toxic contaminants if present.

- ### Bleach Method

Adding 1/8 of a teaspoon (8 drops) of fresh liquid household chlorine bleach (5 to 6% sodium hypochlorite) to every gallon (4 liters) of water will kill most microorganisms. Only household bleach without thickeners, scents, or additives should be used. The use of bleach does not address toxic contamination.

The U. S. Environmental Protection Agency Web site provides additional information about water purification.

- ### Commercial Water Filters

Commercial water filters can effectively filter and purify water contaminated with microorganisms, toxic chemicals, and heavy metals. Their effectiveness depends on design, condition, and proper use. Water filters produced by Seychelle have been used successfully by Church missionaries for many years.

---

[3] Providentliving.org

To learn more and to find local emergency preparedness stores, search the
Internet for water purification and emergency preparedness supplies.
www.seychelle.com
www.katadyn.com

Remember:

- Containers should be emptied and refilled regularly.
- Store water only where potential leakage would not damage your home
  or apartment.
- Protect stored water from light and heat. Some containers may also
  require protection from freezing.
- The taste of stored water can be improved by pouring it back and forth
  between two containers before use.

Water storage containers can be very simple. Water containers such as those
shown, can be purchased or simply using old one liter bottles previously
containing soda will do just fine. Rotate the water regularly and keep it purified.
These containers can be stored most anywhere, in closets, under beds, couches
or furniture. The ability to have ample water for drinking, cooking and
sanitation is most critical

5 Gallon water storage containers

Drinking water in toilet holding tank.

50 Gallon Storage Drum

Pressure relief valve water heater

Water drainage valve

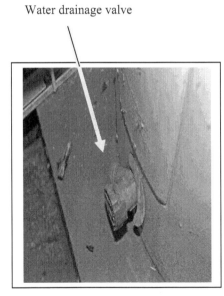

Water heaters are a built in source for drinking water. Every conventional hot water heater has two things in common: an air vent on the top (as shown) and a drain at the bottom. Here is the procedure to access the water:

- Turn off the electric breaker or turn off gas line. Wait to drain the tank until it has had a chance to cool (this may take a few hours). **Draining 130 degree water is very hazardous.**
- Attach a <u>clean hose</u> to the water drain found at the bottom of the heater tank. Be sure it is secure so it does not leak as the valve is opened
- Insert the end of the clean drain hose into the container that you intend to fill. Have someone hold it in place so no water is wasted.
- Slowly open the bottom tank drain valve until you see a small stream of water flowing out. Then open fully.
- Slowly open the top pressure relief valve. No water should flow out of the top valve. If water flows out, close the top valve and check to see that the <u>bottom drain valve is fully opened and not obstructed</u>.
- Allow adequate time for the draining to be completed. Remember it is flowing by gravity only and not under pressure. The water in your house lines may be draining back into the tank (allow time for the upstairs to drain). When flow stops, close the bottom valve, then close the top relief valve.

If normal water service resumes, **you must allow the tank to fill completely before engaging the heater function** (gas or electric). If you turn on the heater element without adequate water, you may destroy the elements or the entire heater. The tank will fill more easily if you open the top relief valve until the tank is completely filled.

In addition to the water heater, there is fresh water in the holding tank of the toilet. It is quite all right; however, you may need to get over the psychological barriers. Even so, it would be a good idea to run it through a filter first. Also, with well water, it is possible for hard water deposits to build up on the inside wall of the tank. Likewise, all that a toilet needs to operate is water. If you have access to a pool, stream or lake nearby, simply fill up the tank with water using a pail or bucket and you are back in business. Take care not to use potable water that could be used for personal consumption. Unless you have an unlimited supply, this would be a foolish use for good drinking water.

Chapter 3

SANITATION

Right away, sanitation will become a problem. There is no stopping *mother nature.* Your specific situation will vary depending on the shelter you choose. Apartment dwellers and those in urban areas depend on sewer pipes. Even if the supply of fresh water ceases, traditional toilets will work for at least for one more flush: there just needs to be water in the holding tank to flush the bowl.

If you have been wise enough to store fresh water in case of emergencies, it would be unwise to use it to refill the toilet bowl. It will not last very long and you may need it for much more important reasons. Besides, the water in the holding tank of the toilet is fresh water. It can be used for drinking. It would be good to have uses for all types of water. "Grey Water" (that used in washing dishes) could be poured in the holding tanks to flush conventional toilets or put in the garden rather than discarding it all together.

A simple solution for dealing with human waste is to have a few buckets on hand along with an ample supply of heavy duty trash bags (lighter weight bags can be doubled up if needed). The previous picture shows a simple make shift toilet. Place the bag in the bucket and secure the edges around the top to assure that it stays in place. A make shift seat can be improvised if necessary with whatever is available. A little improvising would be good here. A close fitting lid will keep the odors at bay. Insecticides and deodorants would also be good to have around.

If you use this method it is important to keep it out of the living area and as sanitized as possible. If this is not done, dysentery, typhoid and diarrhea may develop. Remember the old outhouse in Grandma's back yard? You can even carve a crescent moon on the door.

Be careful not to overfill the liner. The last thing in you want to do is to have a tear due to overweight. Tie the end of the bags or secure them best as possible. Remove the liners often and place them in a larger storage container. This may be a large trash can or drum that could be removed at a later date for permanent disposal.

Under these conditions where clean water and soap is scarce, be extra careful what you touch. Be careful not to put your hands in your mouth, eyes or nose.

If you live in an area where you can dig a hole in the yard, invest in a set of "post-hole diggers". They can be found in any home improvement or quality hardware store. They are intended to dig holes for farm fence posts and they do a very good job. The holes are straight and clean and can be about 24-36"deep. This is just the size needed for a make shift latrine. An improvised seat can be made to cover the hole and provide a bit more comfort. A simple toilet seat cover can be purchased or one can be removed from a non working toilet and placed atop a five (5) gallon paint bucket. Cut the bottom out of the bucket and place it upside down over the hole. Secure the toilet seat over the bucket with whatever material you have and you have all of the luxuries of home, without the flush.

After each use, a little dirt can be thrown in the hole to cover the last deposit. Once the hole is about 1/2 to 2/3 full, remove the bucket and cover it with the rest of the dirt you removed while making the hole;. then dig another one. You could stay in business for quite a long time using this method. Of course, it would be a good idea to surround the area with a tarp or some material that would keep the immediate area private. A small 10'x6' tarp would do just fine. Drive some tall posts in the ground and fasten the tarp to them to create a small square around it. Equipped with a magazine rack on a nearby bush and you may realize that this arrangement is not so bad after all…life is good!

Portable toilets can be purchased on line or camping supply stores. Also, the chemicals used for these toilets can be used for the improvised five gallon toilets described as well. These chemicals will reduce or eliminate most odors associated with the waste and make the whole situation more bearable.

Thetford 25 100 Porta Potti 135

Following the bombing of Germany in World War II, those who survived had to improvise. Here is an illustration on what some of them did to supply the need for toilet paper.

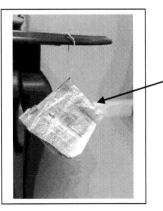

4x4" squares of news paper held by string or yarn.

29

Newsprint was folded, cut into squares and strung on a string. Removing what is needed and wadding it up before use will do the job. If you are using your household toilet by filling the reserve tank with outside water, do not try to flush the news paper. It will certainly clog the drain. It must be disposed of separately.

WATER FOR SANITATION

In many cases, city water will continue to flow during a disaster. Only in extreme circumstances will water tanks and supporting infrastructure be disabled. Assuming that the disaster is not one that contaminates the water system, you are good to go. Otherwise, water storage becomes all too important. Be wise in your usage of fresh water. It is not necessary to use drinking water for many sanitary needs.

Those living in more rural areas will have a few more options when it comes to water. Water wells and septic tanks are the norm. Water wells can be either bored or drilled. The bored wells are larger in diameter and as a result, fairly shallow. Depending on the water table, a bored well can be successful between 20 and 60'. A concrete culvert pipe is placed in the well to prevent cave-ins and to protect the well. In most of these cases access to the top of the well can be gained by removal of the concrete cap placed there. This would grant direct access to the water via rope and bucket. It would be tedious but fresh water could be acquired in this way for sanitation, drinking or bathing. Of course, it would be even better if the well pump could be supplied with local power from a generator. In this case life goes on as usual.

Drilled wells are a different story. The well size is about 6" in diameter and can go very deep; hundreds of feet are customary. The resulting water is usually cleaner and less prone to contamination. The reason for this is because it accesses the lower strata of water which by its very nature has gone through many more natural filtration processes. The problem with this type of well however, is that it would be much more difficult to access the water in times of emergency. After the mechanical devices, the pipe and the submerged pump were removed from the well, the most you could hope to get would be a cup full on the end of a string several hundred feet long. This is not a good option for providing the amounts of fresh water needed.

However, in most cases, there are alternative sources for water in rural areas such as streams, lakes, pools and even ditches. Most all water can be purified unless it has become contaminated though chemical or biological means. Boiling water for ten minutes will most always do the trick.

CHILDREN AND BABIES

Extra care should be taken for children and babies. Always have an extra supply of sanitary wipes on hand. Before the age of disposable diapers, babies wore ones made of cloth (usually cotton). The soiled diapers were rinsed and placed in a bucket with a tight lid and a disinfectant, then washed in a washing machine. Many people concerned about the abundance of diapers in landfills, are using cloth diapers once again. They are not difficult to purchase in specialty stores or on line. Keep a supply of at least 3 dozen on hand.

If no washing machine is available, rinse and wash the diapers the best you can. Then, put them in a big pot of water and boil them for at least ten minutes to steralize. This can be done over a fire if necessary. It is important to be sure that they are in a "rolling boil" for at least ten minutes. This will kill all bacteria including e coli.

Chapter 4

CHILDREN

An emergency situation can become increasingly complicated when a family has small children. More complicated it may be, impossible to handle it certainly is not. The old adage holds true, "an ounce of prevention is worth a pound of cure". By taking the time to prepare in three key areas, you'll be better equipped to handle life for your kids when it's anything but normal.

FOOD

While adults can adapt and accept (however reluctantly) an abrupt change in diet, children will have a more difficult time eating unfamiliar food. In our house, it only took two days of power outage before my 4 year old was crying for favorite foods that I wasn't able to prepare. Always have a supply of familiar food set aside specifically for children and make sure you can prepare it with the emergency supplies you have on hand. Try a few of those meals ahead of time and make sure they're things your kids will enjoy. By doing so, you'll quickly learn what you can and can't do and what your kids will and won't eat. Here are a couple of tips for preparing meals for kids.

- Children are more likely to eat a meal when they've helped prepare it. Give them a chance to become invested in the meal by stirring the ingredients, mixing, pouring, or placing.
- Meal preparation can be made more fun when you're cooking over a fire. This will require caretakers to stress a bit. Eight year old boys may be more interested in leaping over the fire than sitting quietly beside it but they'll eat the food that's been prepared "cave man style".
- Never underestimate the joy of art in cooking. Makeshift sandwiches can be cut into interesting shapes, ketchup can decorate the plate in the shape of a heart or a sunshine, carrot sticks can be stacked like Lincoln logs, and creative presentation may help your kids dive into their dish.
- Present options. In an emergency situation, children can feel disoriented by the lack of normalcy. Give them a sense of control by giving them choices in their meals.

SLEEP

In many emergency situations, sleeping schedules and arrangements will have to be altered. When your home suffers a power outage children may have difficulty sleeping in the dark. They may be reluctant to sleep alone. They may refuse to sleep at all. When your babies refuse to catch the zzz's that are overtaking you, try this.

- Provide a light source. Battery operated reading lights, small flashlights, glow sticks, etc. may give your child the reassurance to relax.

- Try an adventure. When you still have daylight, set up a tent in the living room (or the backyard in comfortable weather). Sleeping just became camping and the child afraid of sleeping in a big dark bedroom may have an easier time sleeping in a cozy tight space.
- Accept that a change in sleeping patterns or situation is not permanent. You're in survival mode, so are the kids. Try to be patient with their fears or insistence. They're struggling to adjust, the same way you are.

- One great alternative for lighting is to use solar powered yard lights. This is not what they were intended for but they work great. They can be purchased at home improvement stores. Leave them in a place where they can soak up the sunlight during the day and you can move them to the kids' room at night to provide safe and effective light.

RECREATION

When kids no longer have access to TVs, computers, or other electronic devices it's time to get back to the basics.
- Outdoor playtime! Take a walk, ride a bike, play tag, hit a ball, visit the park, relax in the shade.
- Enjoy art activities. Dust off the crayons, pull out the play dough, have a paper airplane throwing contest, draw with chalk in the driveway.
- Play board games.
- Read books together.
- Clean. If we're cleaning, we're not whining about boredom. We may be whining about cleaning instead but at least you'll have a spotless space at the end of it.
- Organize. Take the opportunity to go through closets, organize toys, throw out, renew, recycle, and rejuvenate!

The most important thing to remember is that your attitude in a crisis situation will guide your children's attitude. If you are afraid, irritated, or panicked the children will take their cue from you. In reverse, if you are positive, energized, organized and calm, your children will think that life may be a little different than normal but it's not a bad different, in fact, it may even be a cool different.

Chapter 5

Electrical Power

The loss of electrical power is a common disruption following a disaster.

The most obvious source for the temporary supply of electricity to your home are generators. They come in countless sizes capacities and prices. The small portable types are the easiest to have around the house. They should be in a well ventilated area.

How much power do you need in the case of emergency? Only after this determination is made should you go shopping for a generator. Let's go through an exercise.

In the case of an emergency, what can you do without? Even though you may feel that a hot shower is critical, it is something you can do without if you have to. Having every light on in the house, using the electric stove top, the TV and stereo may be nice but it is not critical When considering the things that take up the most power in your home, hot water heaters, clothes dryers, ovens and stove tops are tops on the list.

Unless you have the financial resources to provide large and expensive generators to supply these items, it is more practical to consider the conservative approach to what your power needs may be. What are the critical things?

Critical systems:
- Refrigerator
- Freezer
- Selected lighting (for security)
- Pilot light ignition (for gas furnaces or stove tops) Gas furnaces can be run intermittently if sufficient power is provided to the blower.
- One or two luxury items (radio, TV)
- Well pump (if applicable)
- Selected outlets for charging cell phones, etc.

DETERMINING THE LOAD

The trick for determining the power needed on critical systems is to determine what the total amperage draw at any one time might be. In other words, if all of the items you have plugged in are running at the same time, how much power will it take? The total amperage draw (at peak) plus about 20% is the capacity you will need when considering a generator. It is common for those who purchase generators to believe they are capable of much more than they can do. For example, a 5500 watt generator will effectively generate 45 amps for 110 voltage and 25 amps for 220 voltages, that's all.

At typical light bulb is 100 watts. Typical house current is 110 volts.

Here is a rule of thumb:

The conversion of Watts to Amps is governed by the equation:

Amps = Watts/Volts

For example 100 watts/110 volts = .91 amp (1)

Therefore, a 5500 watt generator will produce 50 amps at 110v, and 25 amps for 220 volts:

- **110 volts (5500/110=50) ,**
  * Reduce by 10% (4950/110=45 amps)

- **220 volts (5500/220= 25amps)**
  * Reduce by 10% (4950/220= 22.5)

* Note: Practical electrical output for generators is regularly overrated by the manufacturer. The ratings are based on "surge" power which will not usually be generated under normal operations. It would be a good idea to reduce the advertised rating by at least 10% for this reason.

BLACK OUT/GREY OUT

One of the most damaging things that you can do is to "starve" your electrical devices from needed power. Providing less power than is required is called a "grey out". **A "black out" is no power; a grey out gives some but not enough.** Insufficient power can destroy motors on refrigerators and other appliances. Don't do it! If you hear the motor energize but not turn (it may sound like a low "hum") and may be an indication that it is getting energy but not enough. Turn it off quickly. This could be an indication of "grey out" and could damage the motor.

This can happens when you ask the generator to provide more power than it is capable of. The amount of power drawn depends on the amount of breakers you have turned on in the panel it is feeding. It may be that you may only be able to run one or two items at a time. Turn all of the other breakers off. If you do not do this, you will soon be purchasing new appliances when the lights come back on. Be careful to use the formula provided along with the load (electrical) chart to determine the amount of power you need to provide.

Consider the following:

- **110 volt** devices

Typically, refrigerators will draw around 500 watts (see chart). Use the formula to determine the amount of amps it will draw: watts/voltage = amps. Therefore, 500 watts/110 volts = 4.55 or 5 amps. OK, with the refrigerator running you can run two or three other appliances of similar current draw, comfortably on a 5500 watt generator.

37

It is important to remember that there can be variations in the power usage stated by the manufacturer. Therefore, it is important to supply 10-20% more power than the anticipated draw.

- **220 volt devices**

Ovens are usually placed on a 50 amp circuit breaker. Typically, you would not want to supply this appliance on a small generator unless there was nothing else on it. Clothes dryers will usually pull around 20-25 amps. You can see from the previous calculation that the 5500 watt generator would be sufficient to supply adequate current for either the oven or dryer by itself but not much more. Remember, don't push it.

This is why it is important to consider what is absolutely needed and what can be done by other means. Consider purchasing gas appliances driven by propane or natural gas. The electric fan on a gas furnace would pull very little current (750 watts or 7 amps). The ignition switches for the pilot lights on gas stove tops can be run with minimum power. In worse case scenarios, you can do without an oven. Go to the camping department of your favorite store. Purchase a cast iron Dutch Oven and learn the art of cooking with it over charcoal or the coals of a fire. Clothes can be washed by hand and hung out to dry; just like your grandma.

ON SITE GENERATORS

- **Direct supply:** This is the simplest way to attach the generator to the appliance. The generator is running in a well ventilated area and an extension cord is connected to the appliance. All generators need to be connected to an appropriate ground. It is fast and simple. However, it can only run one or two items at a time depending on how many receptacles there are on the generator.

Generac GP 5500

- **BACK FED:** This is a process where the generator is attached to a custom made extension cord. One end fits into the supply side of the generator and the other end is attached to the female supply receptacle of a 220 volt appliance like a clothes dryer. **This option should not used for any generator supplying more than 5500 watts.** Power is fed from the generator to the dryer receptacle which then feeds the main electrical panel in a "reverse flow" configuration. This is why it is called 'back fed".

$\Longrightarrow$ **See reference section for Generator back fed procedure.**

This can be hazardous but in the worse case scenarios, it may be an option. If you choose this option, make the connectors well in advance and practice the procedure so you have it memorized. The biggest hazard is that you may have an energized male connector which will violate every safe electrical practice taught. As long as this energized male connector stays in the female dryer connector it will not present a hazard but this option must be considered carefully.

Also, this option must not be considered unless there is a main disconnect switch on the main service panel to the house. Extreme effort should be taken to assure that the power delivered to the panel by the generator is not present when the main power is restored.

If you do not have a main disconnect switch at the entry service panel, do not consider this option. If you are back feeding power in to the main panel while the main electrical supply is restored, a fire or worse may result. Also, if you do not interrupt the circuit from the main feed, you are energizing the lines that lead from the home. This could jeopardize the safety of those working on the downed lines.

With that being said, the procedure is as follows: The generator is connected to the dryer service line or any other high voltage service receptacle. All of the circuit breakers in the main service panel are switched off including the main service breaker disconnecting the main panel form the outside supply lines. Once every breaker is switched off, turn on only the critical ones needed after the generator is properly connected. Do not exceed the calculated supply of power to the panel as previously discussed.

Remember that the item that you want to energize may be only one item on the entire circuit. The ones not needed should be switched off. This may be a challenge if an electrical schematic is not provided by the installing electrician. It is almost never provided in a residential setting. Work on the "runs" of the circuits in advance by plugging many different things in an area where you can see the light or hear the noise of the item running and turn off the circuit of choice. It may take some time but you will eventually be able to determine all of the receptacles and light fixtures it provides. In many cases, a circuit is dedicated to a specific area to service both receptacles and overhead lights to save wire. Other circuits are run independently for receptacles and light fixtures so as to not leave you in the dark if one or the other is tripped. This could be a fun family activity for the kids to be the eyes and ears for dad at the breaker panel. For most electrical codes, dedicated circuits are required for major appliances such as refrigerators or freezers. These circuits should be easy to locate. Simply begin tripping the breakers one by one until you find the one that turns it off. Label that breaker and move on to the next.

GENERATOR FUEL POSSIBILITIES

Basic fuel choices are propane, natural gas, diesel, and gasoline. The following chart provides contrast of those fuel choices and some of their relative qualities.

FUEL	STORABILITY	SAFETY
Propane	No known limit	Good
Natural Gas	No known limit	Good
Diesel	1 + years w/ treatment	Good
Gasoline	6 months w/ treatment	Explosive Vapor

Other notes that may help you decide which fuel is best for your situation:

- **Gasoline:** Gasoline is the most unstable and difficult to store. If left in the machine for an extended period of time, it will coagulate making it difficult to start. The use of a fuel stabilizer is critical for storage. However, it is the most commonly available due to its relative cost and availability.
- **Diesel:** This fuel is readily available, easy to store, has good storage life and is relatively safe but cost more at the pump. Diesel generators are usually more expensive too but are also more heavy duty and robust. My experience is that they will perform better and last longer and are worth the additional cost when purchasing one if you plan to keep it around.
- **Natural gas:** This will likely be a special order item. It is clean burning, usually requires less maintenance and has much longer service life than its gasoline alternative. Natural gas pipelines might remain operational even during a regional disaster due to the nature of how they are delivered over interstate underground pipeline systems.

- **Propane (LP):** A generator using this fuel might have to be special ordered. LP is clean burning, easily stored in pressurized cylinders but is commonly delivered by truck; if transportation is interrupted supplies may disappear. This fuel is a very dangerous alternative and must NEVER be stored inside. Propane fuel is heavier than air and if accidently released, will linger low to the floor where it can easily be ignited by pilot lights from water heaters or other appliances. Many cases of death and injury have been reported due to accidental LP explosions.

Whatever your fuel choice is, you will need to know its availability and how it can be used for maximum efficiency. Fuel-use planning requires immediate evaluation of what electrical items are necessary and which are not. This evaluation must involve all the adults in the family in order to carry out whatever decisions are made.

How long will your fuel last? (Approximate)

(30 gal of fuel @ ½ gal per hour consumption)

2 hours on 2 off:	5 days	(6 gal/ day)
2 hours on 3 off	7 ½ days	(4 gal/day)
2 hours on 4 off	10 days	(3 gal/day)

The chart above demonstrates how increasing the off time can stretch fuel supplies. Check the fuel consumption tables for your system; calculate your fuel storage, then using various on/off intervals compute how long your supply would last.

Other emergency generator factors to consider:

- Become familiar with your generator's capabilities before it is needed. Keep operator's manual in an easily accessible place.
- Run your generator once per month (under load) to keep it running properly.
- Do not operate an electric stove or cook top on the generator unless you have a large supply of fuel and you are sure that the generator can handle the load.
- Do not store a generator with diesel or gasoline in the fuel system. Install a fuel shut off valve. After testing the system, shut the valve and allow the generator to continue running until all fuel in the line has been consumed

and it stops on its own. This procedure is not necessary with LP or natural gas units.

- During operation it should be in a secure location with adequate ventilation.
- Prior to running the generator, carefully gather all items that must be recharged (batteries, flashlights, cell phones, power tools) and prepare them to be hooked up immediately when the generator is started. When they are charged, take them off line to reduce load and fuel consumption.
- Remember to monitor generator oil.
- The greater electrical load placed on the generator, the more fuel will be consumed per hour
- Electric water heaters and heat pumps draw large amounts of power. Formulate a plan to use those only when necessary, and only in accordance with your plan. Water can be heated once per day or every other day and bathing/washing times can be carefully planned.

A FEW CONSIDERATIONS ON REFRIGERATION:

- Remember that every time that you open the door to the refrigerator, you are releasing the cool air thereby reducing the time it will take to thaw its contents
- If the disaster will likely continue for more than a few days, you should plan on using as much refrigerator contents as possible before they spoil.
- Plan on refrigeration being available only for a number of days, estimate how long you can generate power, then plan what will be used each day so as little as possible goes to waste.
- Understand that when you run out of fuel you may not be able to replenish that supply.
- Heavy/dense items such as meat remain frozen longer.
- If the door remains closed, a freezer can keep most items sufficiently cold even if the system operates for two hours at a time.
- If the freezer is an upright, move food toward the bottom (where it is colder) as much as possible.
- A bank of batteries can be used to power AC (110volt) appliances.

Inverters such as this one shown can be attached to a bank of batteries to power critical electrical need for things like a refrigerator or freezer. They are not necessarily expensive and can come in handy when you absolutely positively have to have electricity. They are easily found on line. It is important however when considering this option that it may take a lot of batteries to do the job if you are planning for them to run for a long time.

1250 Watt Power Inverter 12 Volt by AIMS
Model #:PWRINV1250W

⇨ *(See the chapter on Communications for explanation of Battery banks)*

TRANSFER SWITCHES

Transfer switches are the preferred devises for applying local electrical service to your home, mainly because they are very safe and easy to use.

Manual transfer switch panel
Switch lever
Main Service Panel
Pigtail connector "to generator"

Manual: This device is very simple to install and operate. A "pigtail" hangs from the switch which is connected to the generator when needed. The main switch is then transferred from external to local power by simply moving the lever upward. It automatically disconnects the offsite power, eliminating the problem discussed in the previous scenario on "back feeding". It is also important to switch off all circuits that are not critical. It is easy to ask for more

43

power than the generator can supply. Use the chart provided and do not overload the generator: remember the discussion on "grey out!"

In the specific case previously shown, this switch is wired to a separate and independent panel which feeds critical circuits in the home. When the regular power is reestablished, the remainder of the circuits becomes active. The switch is simply returned to the off position reconnecting power from the "pigtail" going to the generator to the main service panel on the right. Also, in this case there are no problems associated with back feeding when the commercial power is reestablished.

Automatic: An automatic transfer switch is one where the drop of external electrical service is automatically detected. A switch is then energized starting the generator automatically. The generator is typically large enough to supply the electrical service panel "as is" when the power is lost. Therefore, it would have to be large enough to supply the needs of the entire house. These generators are usually large and expensive but nevertheless a great option.

Photo Shown: Generac 200 Amp Power Manager Load Shedding Service Disconnect Transfer Switch

Use the following chart to be sure that you are staying within the acceptable levels of power supplied to power needed. If you wish to supply the entire power needs of the home and to remain in the lap of luxury regardless of the existence of the external power grid, you will need to invest in a full time automatic generator.

GE 20 K Home Generator Systems, Modal#: 040331GE

Beware, these puppies are great, but they will set you back on the budget. When purchasing the generator, tell the sales consultant what you want it to do and hopefully they will put you on the right product. **The following is a simple device that can be used as a multipurpose apparatus which will read the actual power draw in addition to providing surge protection. Other commercial devices are available as well. This will take the guess work out of the calculations needed to provide adequate power.**

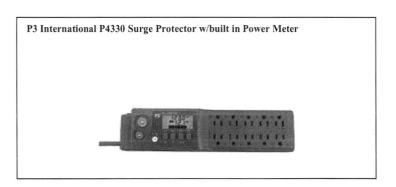

P3 International P4330 Surge Protector w/built in Power Meter

TYPICAL USEAGE CHART FOR HOUSEHOLD APPLIANCES

Dishwasher	700W	Microwave Oven	1200W
Garbage Disposal	200W	Refrigerator	500W
Range (8" element)	2000W	Water Heater (Electric)	4500W
Mixer	200W	Mixer	200W
Frying Pan	1200W	Coffee Maker	1500W
Toaster Oven	1200W	Toaster	1000W
Waffle Iron	1000W	Stereo	200W
Radio	50W	TV	500W
Personal Computer	700W	Hair Dryer	1500W
Sump Pump	1000W	Electric Blanket	500W
Dehumidifier	1000W	Fan	250W
Vacuum Cleaner	900W	Iron	1200W
Dryer (Electric)	5000W	Dryer (Gas)	500W
Washer	700W	Electric Heat Strips	1500W
Room Air Conditioner	1200W	Well Pump	750W
Stand Alone Freezer	500W	Furnace Fan	750W

45

AN IDEA FOR EMERGENCY LIGHTING

One great alternative for interior emergency lighting that is safe and effective is to employ the services for something that has another purpose all together: a **Solar Power Walk Light.** These are the ones that you will see around homes and businesses to illuminate the walkways and entrances. What makes these so effective is that they are completely self-sufficient. They need no wiring or electrical power of any kind. Being solar powered, they can be placed in the yard during the daylight hours in their normal place, by the flowers or just stuck upright in a box. The solar panel is located on the topside so it is important that the top faces full sunlight. There is also a built in "photocell" which turns the light on automatically when it gets dark. You can purchase a set of six for under $20.

In concept, you can have a readymade supply of emergency lighting working every day in the yard. When the need arises, go outside and pull one up: just like picking carrots from the garden. The LED bulb is not very bright (it is not meant to be) but would do as much or more than a candle but with none of the risk associated with an open flame in the house. They would be great for night light in the kid's room if placed in a safe location out of their reach.

(Light shown in image: Hampton Bay 611715)

Chapter 6

MEDICAL

Note: The contents of this section are not medical advice, and should not be construed as providing medical advice or treatment. This section is intended to raise individual awareness about basic health and nutritional issues in an environment of sudden scarcity of medical services. The authors therefore recommend that individuals and families undertake their own research and make contact with licensed medical practitioners to prescribe medicines or treatments for any maladies or injuries whenever possible.

As you read this book, your life is probably still very much as you have always known it to be, where most everything you are accustomed to using still works as usual. Large scale disruptions change all of that, therefore most of your former experiences with how things "work" may at some point no longer be very helpful. Thriving in the new environment will require you to think in terms of possibilities, basic needs, and principles. **The wheel is the wheel, fire is still hot, and water flows downhill.** Adapt what you already know by slowing down and thinking about the most beneficial course of action.

Become determined to use your present knowledge of medical principles to:
- Maintain your present strength.
- Prevent injuries.
- Minimize illness or injuries that do occur.
- Make the best of serious problems that might in the long run be far beyond your control.

Under normal circumstances, balanced meals easily provide proper vitamins and nutrients necessary to maintain health. As you remain in your home when the surrounding world has been drastically altered, your diet will change. Scarcity of various foods may well become the norm. If you are prepared with multivitamins, that will afford time for you to work out alternative means of maintaining basic nourishment. Nutrition related disease can be every bit as devastating as wounds.

MINOR INJURIES

Treat them immediately! You must take extra care to avoid injuries whenever possible. When professional medical care is not available, preventing personal injury is vital. What would otherwise be a quick stop in a local emergency room might become a life-threatening crisis due to subsequent infection.

- In order to handle minor injuries, you <u>must</u> have functional first aid supplies and basic reference material.
- First aid reference books are necessary so you are not forced to guess at any basic treatment, and possibly make the problem worse. Look up the injury, treat using common sense and according to written guidelines.
- If you are injured (cut, punctured, burned, abraded etc.) treat the injury a soon as possible.

HEAT INJURIES

High temperatures and humidity stress the body's ability to cool itself, and heat illness becomes a special concern during hot weather. **There are three major forms of heat illnesses: heat cramps, heat exhaustion, and heat stroke, with heat stroke being a life threatening condition.** [4]

Heat cramps are muscle spasms which usually affect the arms, legs, or stomach. Frequently they don't occur until sometime later after work, at night or when relaxing. **Heat cramps** are caused by heavy sweating, especially when water is replaced by drinking but not salt or potassium. Although heat cramps can be quite painful, they usually don't result in permanent damage. To prevent them, drink electrolyte solutions such as Gatorade during the day and try eating more fruits like bananas.

Heat Exhaustion is more serious than heat cramps. It occurs when the body's internal air-conditioning system is overworked but hasn't completely shut down. In heat exhaustion, the surface blood vessels and capillaries which originally enlarged to cool the blood collapse from loss of body fluids and necessary minerals. This happens when you don't drink enough fluids to replace what you're sweating away.

The symptoms of heat exhaustion include: headache, heavy sweating, intense thirst, dizziness, fatigue, loss of coordination, nausea, impaired judgment, loss of appetite, hyperventilation, tingling in hands or feet, anxiety, cool moist skin, weak and rapid pulse (120-200), and low to normal blood pressure. Persons suffering these symptoms should be moved to a cool location such as a shaded area or air-conditioned building. Have them lie down with their feet slightly elevated. Loosen their clothing, apply cool, wet clothes or fan them. Have them drink water or electrolyte drinks. Try to cool them down and have them checked by medical personnel. Victims of heat exhaustion should avoid strenuous activity for at least a day and they should continue to drink water to replace lost body fluids.

Heat Stroke is a life threatening illness with a **high death rate**. It occurs when the body has depleted its supply of water and salt and the victim's body temperature rises to deadly levels. A heat stroke victim may first suffer heat cramps and/or the heat exhaustion before progressing into the heat stroke stage but this is not always the case. It should be noted that, **heat stroke is sometimes**

---

[4] United States Marine Corps

mistaken for heart attack. It is therefore very important to be able to recognize the signs and symptoms of heat stroke - and to check for them anytime someone collapses while working in a hot environment.

The early symptoms of heat stroke include a high body temperature (103 degrees F), a distinct absence of sweating (usually), hot red or flushed dry skin; rapid pulse, difficulty breathing; constricted pupils, any and all the signs or symptoms of heat exhaustion such as dizziness, headache, nausea, vomiting or confusion, but more severe, bizarre behavior and high blood pressure. Advanced symptoms may be seizure or convulsions, collapse, loss of consciousness and a body temperature of over 108° F.

It is vital to lower a heat stroke victim's body temperature: Seconds count. Pour water on them, fan them or apply cold packs. Call 911 and get an ambulance on the way as soon as possible. Anyone can suffer a heat illness but by taking a few simple precautions, they can be prevented:

- **Condition yourself for working in hot environments** - start slowly then build up to more physical work. Allow your body to adjust over a few days.
- **Drink lots of liquids.** Don't wait until you're thirsty; by then, there's a good chance you're already on your way to being dehydrated. Electrolyte drinks are good for replacing both water and minerals lost through sweating. Never drink alcohol and avoid caffeinated beverages like coffee and soft drinks.
- **Take a break if you notice you're getting a headache or you start feeling overheated.** Cool off for a few minutes before going back to work.
- **Wear light weight, light colored clothing** when working out in the sun.
- **Take advantage of fans and air-conditioners.**
- **Get enough sleep at night.**
- **With a little <u>caution and common sense</u>, you can avoid heat illnesses.**

COLD INJURIES

Chilblains is a nonfreezing cold injury resulting from repeated, prolonged skin exposure to cold and wet (high humidity) temperatures above freezing.[5] Exposed skin becomes red, tender and hot to the touch and is usually

---

[5] Army Medicine Feb. 2010

accompanied with itching. This can worsen to an aching, prickly (pins and needles) sensation and then numbness. Chilblains can develop in exposed skin in only a few hours. The most commonly affected areas are the ears, nose, fingers and toes.

Immersion Foot/Trench Foot is a nonfreezing injury that results from prolonged exposure to wet conditions between 32–60°. Not maintaining proper hygiene and allowing sweat to accumulate in shoes or gloves will soften the skin, causing tissue loss and often cause infection. These cold and wet conditions constrict blood vessels and the affected areas become cold, swollen, discolored, waxy and are often accompanied by sensations of pins and needles, numbness and then pain. In extreme cases, flesh dies and amputation may be necessary.

Frostnip is the freezing of the top layers of skin tissue and is considered the first degree of frostbite. Frostnip usually results from short-duration exposure to cold air or contact with a cold object such as metal. Exposed skin, such as the cheeks, ears, fingers and wrists are more likely to develop frostnip. The top layer of frozen skin becomes white, waxy and feels hard and rubbery while the deeper tissue is still soft. The affected area feels numb and may become swollen but does not blister. Frozen skin thaws quickly, becoming red and painful with eventual peeling of the skin with complete healing with 10 days and injury is normally reversible.

Frostbite is the actual freezing of skin tissue that can extend through all layers of the skin and actually freeze the muscle and bone. Frozen skin may turn red and then gray-blue with blisters and in worst cases, the skin dies and turns blue-black. At this stage, amputation is often required. Deep frozen skin feels "wooden" to the touch with zero mobility of the affected body part. Instantaneous frostbite can occur when the skin comes in contact with super-cooled liquids, such as fuel, antifreeze, and alcohol, all of which remain liquid at temperatures as low as -40°F.

Hypothermia is a potential life threatening conditions that is defined as the general cooling of the body core temperature below 95°F (normal body temperature is 98.6°F). Hypothermia sets in when the body-heat lost exceeds the body's heat production due to prolonged cold exposure. Although hypothermia is usually associated with cold climates, it can occur at temperatures well above freezing especially when a person is exposed to extended wet conditions.

Signs and symptoms of hypothermia change as body temperature falls. Mental functions typically decline first; marked with declined decision making ability, slurred speech, disorientation, incoherence, irrationality, and possible unconsciousness. Muscle functions deteriorate with shivering, lose of fine motor ability (i.e. unable to complete tasks with hands), progressing to stumbling, clumsiness and falling. In severe cases, shivering ceases and the person exhibits stiffness and inability to move. Pulse and respiration rates decrease progressing to unconsciousness, irregular heartbeat, and death.

Unfortunately, early signs and symptoms of hypothermia can be difficult to recognize and may easily go undetected. A victim may deny he/she is in trouble; believe the symptoms, not the victim.

Dehydration is a lack of water in the body. Most people associate dehydration with hot weather conditions. However, it is very easy to become dehydrated in cold weather and many individuals fail to drink enough liquid and underestimate fluid loss from sweating. Proper hydration is especially important in cold weather as dehydration adversely affects the body's resistance to cold injury, increasing the chance cold weather injuries. Remember that proper hydration is essential to supplying fuel and energy to body parts to facilitate heat production.

Risk Factors: Understanding the contributing factors of cold weather injuries provides a better understanding of the best methods on how to combat the cold. Environmental factors including temperature, wind, rain, immersion and altitude; work load; duration of cold/wet exposure and individual risk factors such as physical fitness, fatigue, health, prior history of cold injury, use of medications, alcohol, nicotine and poor nutrition can all contribute to cold weather injuries.

Prevention: Individuals can work and play in cold environments if they are properly prepared and understand basic control measures to prevent cold weather injuries.

Keep body warm:
- Keep moving by exercising big muscles (arms, legs) to keep warm.
- Avoid alcohol use as it impairs the body's ability to shiver and gives a false sense of warmth.
- Avoid all tobacco products as they decrease blood circulation to the skin.
- Eat all meals to maintain energy.

- Drink water or warm non-caffeinated/non-alcoholic fluids to prevent dehydration. Drinking warm liquids like tea and hot chocolate contain sugar provides energy to help the body generate additional heat.
- Limit the amount of time outside on extremely cold days.

Wear proper clothing

- Several layers of loose clothing, rather than one or two "bulky" layers. Air is trapped between these layers and acts as insulation against the cold. The layers can also be removed if you become too hot to prevent sweating. Loose clothing allows the blood to circulate to the extremities.
- Change wet, damp clothes immediately.
- **Protect feet:**
  o Change damp socks immediately.
  o Use food powder to help absorb moisture.
  o Wear overshoes to keep shoes and socks clean and dry.
- **Protect hands:**
  o Wear gloves, mittens or gloves/mittens with inserts to avoid frostbite injuries.
  o Keep gloves/mittens clean and dry; change damp gloves immediately.
  o Warm hands under clothes if they become numb.
  o Avoid skin contact with snow, fuel or bare metal that has been exposed to the cold for extended periods.
- **Protect head, face and ears:**
  o Wear a hat. As much as 70 percent or more of the body's heat is lost through an uncovered head and a hat reduces the amount of body heat that escapes from your head.
  o Cover face and ears with scarf to prevent frostbite injuries. In combination, a hat and scarf protect the skin and retain body heat.
  o Warm face and ears by covering them with your hands but do not rub face or ears.
  o Wear sunscreen.
  o Exercise facial muscles to help maintain circulation.
- **Protect friends and family:**
  o Watch for signs of frostbite and other cold weather injuries in others.
  o Ask about and assist with re-warming of feet, hands, ears or face.
  o Immediately treat persons showing any sign/symptom of cold injury.
  o Remove sick, injured and wounded individuals from the cold as they are very susceptible to cold injuries.

COMMON SICKNESSES THAT CAN KILL

The 20th century saw dramatic advances in the treatment and prevention of many diseases. If our civilization is disrupted; however, these diseases may become more common and indeed are still found to be endemic in some parts of the world. The best defense against these classical killers is good personal hygiene, adequate nourishment, proper immunization and not being bottled up with large numbers of other people in close proximity.

A few examples of common diseases follow.
- Measles
- Diarrheal diseases,
- Acute Respiratory Infections
- Malaria is often serious among refugee and displaced populations.
- Communicable diseases such as meningococcal meningitis, hepatitis, typhoid fever, and relapsing fever are common in refugee camps.

Factors that will increase risk of illness:
- Crowded, close quarters with poor sanitation
- Inadequate clean water
- Inadequate shelter
- All of the above improve conditions for spread of disease. Malnutrition and infection work together to produce extreme danger for the aged and very young.

Measles
Inadequate immunization, high rates of under-nutrition and vitamin A deficiency have contributed to spreading. Measles continues to be a leading cause of death among refugee children. Measles may lead to a vitamin A deficiency, thus weakening the person further.

Diarrheal diseases
Diarrheal diseases are a serious threat because of inadequate water supply (quality and quantity), and insufficient or improperly designed sanitation facilities. More persons have died from this kind of disease than have been killed by direct action in warfare.

Cholera

Cholera has always been a killer. Polluted water sources, improperly sanitized/shared water containers and cooking utensils/pots, lack of soap, improper storage of leftovers and contaminated food are significant infection risk factors.

Acute Respiratory Infections

Acute respiratory infections are often the leading cause of death among displaced person populations. Children suffer disproportionally more than others. These infections may often be avoided or by improving shelter and basic nutrition.

Tuberculosis (TB)

TB remains a worldwide health risk. Crowded living accommodations and poor nutrition may foster the spread of the disease. Although not usually a leading cause of death during the initial phase, TB often evolves into a critical problem. Many TB patients are not compliant with medication administration instructions and thus are never healed, although symptoms may be suppressed. At certain stages, TB is highly contagious and some strains attack very quickly.

Malaria

Malaria continues to be a severe problem in many areas and has been increasing in some localities. Malnutrition and anemia may be directly related to recurrent or persistent malaria infection or may compound the effects of malaria and lead to high mortality. The presence of large mosquito populations and stagnant or standing water are perfect for establishing or spreading malaria.

Hepatitis

Hepatitis has not been among the most common diseases reported in refugee and displaced populations worldwide; however, where access to adequate supplies of clean water has been severely limited, it is a problem.

Meningitis

Overcrowding and limited medical care contribute to outbreaks of meningococcal meningitis. Children less than 5 years of age are at greatest risk for meningitis but it may also occur among older children and adults, particularly in densely populated environments.

Typhus

Deadly risk factors include:

- Exposure to rat fleas or rat feces
- Exposure to other animals (such as cats, opossums, raccoons, skunks, and squirrels)

Symptoms of typhus may include:

- Chills
- Cough
- Delirium
- High fever (104 degrees Fahrenheit)
- Joint pain (*arthralgia*)
- Lights that appear very bright; light may hurt the eyes
- Low blood pressure
- Rash that begins on the chest and spreads to the rest of the body (except the palms of the hands and soles of the feet)
- Severe headache
- Severe muscle pain
- Stupor

COMMON PARASITIC DISEASES
(Human and animal borne)

Parasites are living things that use other living things for food and a place to live. They can be contracted from contaminated food, water, bug bites, or sexual contact. Parasitic diseases may cause mild discomfort or be quite deadly. Parasites range in size from tiny, one-celled organisms called protozoa to worms that can be seen with the naked eye.

- Contaminated water supplies – (Giardia infections)
- Cats can transmit toxoplasmosis, (dangerous to pregnant women)
- Malaria common in many areas of the world.

Drink only water you know is safe. Prevention is especially important. There are no vaccines for parasitic diseases. In a situation of scarcity it is unlikely that medicines are available to treat parasitic infections.

SERIOUS ACCIDENTAL INJURIES

- Simple fractures
- Burns (become infected very easily)
- Head injuries (may cause concussion or worse)

This would be the time to use your network of contacts and bring in a professional if possible. Any number of good books are available that will help a non-medical person to give basic support until professionals can be brought in. *Have one on hand well in advance of the need.*

COMMON VITAMIN/DIETARY DEFICIENCY DISORDERS

Basic disease prevention often depends on doing a just few things right consistently.

Vitamin C Deficiency (scurvy)

Common symptoms: Teeth loosen, hair falls out, vision is affected and is caused by a lack of vitamin C. If you have a reasonable supply of vitamin C in your preparedness supplies, you will be able to avoid scurvy by taking even small doses regularly. The supply of vitamins will give you time to plant a garden or locate necessary supplies.
Basic causes: Scurvy is rare in stable populations in developing countries but many outbreaks have occurred in displaced and famine-affected populations in recent years. Scurvy is commonly associated with extended time in refugee camps during which vitamin C is not part of the regular diet. A historical note, this disease was very common among European peasant populations before basic nutrition was understood.
Basic precautions: Green vegetables or other foods having significant vitamin C content.

Pellagra

Common symptoms: Mental confusion/delusions, loss of appetite, skin rash, rough tongue surface, diarrhea, digestive trouble, irritated/inflamed mucus membranes, inability to concentrate, scaly sores on a person's skin.
Basic causes: Vitamin B-3 deficiency, and/or insufficient niacin or tryptophan in the diet. This may also occur if the body fails to absorb these nutrients for some physical reason, in conjunction with certain gastrointestinal diseases. Pellagra is often found in groups where corn composes a large part of their diet.

Basic precautions: A regular diet including protein usually supplies sufficient Vitamin B3 to maintain the body's needs, beef liver, brewer's yeast, lean meats, poultry, fish, eggs, cheese, soybeans, nuts, whole grains, green vegetables, cooked dried beans and milk (non- or low fat milk) all provide sources of niacin and niacin amide. Vegetables should be baked, steamed or prepared as stir-fry to retain vitamin B3.

Beriberi

Common symptoms: Common symptoms associated with beriberi include difficulty walking, decreased sensation in the hands and feet, decreased muscle function or paralysis of the lower legs, mental confusion, difficulty with speech, pain, rapid eye movements, vomiting, shortness of breath during exertion, increased heart rate and lower leg swelling.

Basic causes: Lack of thiamine, or vitamin B-1. In the United States, beriberi is most commonly seen among people who abuse alcohol.

Basic precautions: A person eating a healthy balanced, basic diet should ingest sufficient thiamine.

Rickets

Usual symptoms: Rickets include delayed growth, muscle weakness, pain centered in the vertebrae or spinal bones, pelvis and legs, cavities and problems with teeth structure.

Basic causes: Vitamin D deficiency. Child bones become soft and easily fractured. Vitamin D is a vital part of the mechanism that enables of calcium and phosphorus absorption.

Basic precautions: Since it is (generally) caused by a nutritional deficiency, increasing consumption of vitamin D and calcium usually helps restore health. The unborn can suffer terribly from vitamin deficiencies, thus expectant mothers must receive the best diet possible. Treatments may vary.

Time is the friend to those prepared with a supply of seeds and the will to cultivate a good sized garden. Time is the enemy of those who simply take their vitamins and wait for someone to come and rescue them. In a regional disaster, time may run out for those of a passive disposition.

HEALTH ISSUES REGARDING IN HOME ENTRAPMENT

A safe room/shelter from which you cannot escape that is without food and water is of little worth. If minimal supplies are positioned in the safe storm shelter, the probability of surviving entrapment increases considerably. The shelter need not duplicate other readiness supplies; rather these can be stored in the room and removed as necessary for other use.

- **Sanitation** ⟶ *See the Chapter on Sanitation*

- **Respiratory illness prevention**

  o If conditions are damp symptoms may worsen
  o Minimal first aid supplies should be in this area to treat transient symptoms

- **Psychological issues**

  o **Claustrophobia**: is a psychological condition that is manifested by extreme fear of enclosed spaces. If a member of your family has this condition, they would likely find entrapment to be very traumatic.
  o **Boredom:** Consider having a few board games and a battery powered radio in your kit to break the monotony of confinement.
  o **Cabin fever:** This is generally defined as stress resulting from/during confinement, captivity, or isolation. It is an emotional state, characterized by irritability, temper instability, distress, or depression. A person experiencing this condition will generally improve quickly once the confinement is over.
  o **Temperament:** Type A personalities will not do well during entrapment. Waiting (mostly in the dark) is depressing and frustrating. Patience and hope would be very valuable to calm everyone's fears.
  o **Sincere prayer** has been found to bring comfort and hope to many in such desperate situations

- **Heat/cold injury**

  o Water on a towel or wash cloth will help to cool when applied to forehead or chest
  o A few blankets might be needed in cold climates to prevent cold injury. Body heat or chemical warm packs will be the only sources of heat. *WARNING: No heater or device that produces flame or fumes of any kind may be used in a confined room due to <u>carbon monoxide which is fatal</u>.*

- **Dehydration**
  - Next to physical injury from the building collapse, dehydration the most dangerous and immediate threat to life in an entrapment
  - Each person in the room must drink at least 1/2 gallon of water per day.
  - Positioning as little as three gallons of water per probable occupant should be sufficient in all but the most extreme situation. This would provide sufficient hydration to maintain life for several days.

MEDICAL SUMMARY

- Avoid injuries, be careful and protect yourself.
- If injured treat immediately.
- Develop a back up network so a medical professional can be consulted if necessary.
- Eat as much of a balanced diet as possible, even if the amount you can eat is very little. Balance may be more helpful than quantity.
- Be vigilant for manifestations of diseases and do not assume that minor troubles are insignificant.

FIRST AID SUPPLIES

Author's note: Expand your vision when it comes to the size of a first aid kit and purchase a plastic bin or large portable container. Medical supplies are not something you want to be without when they are needed. Put together an emergency kit (Information supplied by the American Red Cross and FEMA)

Basic First Aid Kit: Assemble a first aid kit for your home and one for each car.

- Sterile adhesive bandages in assorted sizes
- Butterfly bandages
- Hydrogen peroxide
- Betadine or alcohol
- Neosporin or other anti-bacterial ointment
- Medical tape
- Cleansing agent/soap
- Latex gloves (2 pairs)

- Sunscreen
- 2-inch sterile gauze pads (4-6)
- Triangular bandages (3)
- Heat wraps (instant)
- Elastic bandages (for sprains)
- Ice packs (instant)
- Aloe (for burns)
- 2-inch sterile roller bandages (3 rolls)
- Scissors
- Tweezers
- Needle
- Moistened towelettes
- Thermometer
- Tongue blades (for splints)
- Tube of petroleum jelly or other lubricant
- Eye wash
- Anti-fungal cream
- Hydrocortisone or other anti-itch cream

Non-Prescription Drugs

- Aspirin or non aspirin pain reliever (Children's also)
- Cough and cold medication (include cough drops)
- Multi-Vitamins
- Vitamin C
- Benadril (allergic reaction or insect stings)
- Anti-nausea medication
- Anti-diarrhea medication
- Antacid
- Syrup of Ipecac (use to induce vomiting if advised by the Poison Control Center)
- Laxative
- Activated charcoal (use if advised by the Poison Control Center
- Other medications for your particular families needs
- Prescription Medication (always have 3 month supply on hand)

My family has always been good about advance preparation for emergency situations. I have stored medical supplies in the basement for years. We recently opened up an ammo can where I had stored some supplies years ago. The container had a liquid (hydrogen peroxide) that had sweated and introduced moisture into the sealed can. As a result all of the contents were destroyed. It is important therefore, to store the needed supplies properly and check on them on a regular basis.

It was fortunate that the damage was discovered before they were actually needed. Imagine the frustration that would have been felt if the can had been opened in a time of need and to find it all worthless. Medical supplies are not something that you want to be short of. This is one item that you need to be very generous in keeping stocked. Get more than you think you need. The reason may be for something unexpected like the loss of items to damage in an ammo can. Of course, it would be smarter not to put a liquid in a sealed ammo can: we do learn lesson hard sometimes!

Chapter 9

COMMUNICATIONS

Co-author Andrew Jones atop his 100' ham radio tower installing a 40 meter mono-band ham radio antenna.

The first six pages of this chapter is an expert taken from our companion book: Evacuation: A Family Guide To the 21 Century due to the identical purposes for the need to communicate. The following pages deal with longer term issues concerning communications while in a stationary emergency situation.

COMMUNICATING TO THE OUTSIDE WORLD

Keeping the family safe and staying current on local information requires communications. Cell phones may or may not be operational during times of crisis. They may shut down by sheer volume or by government intervention. The best communication options are HAM radios (range up to 10-20 miles (simplex) depending on conditions, GMRS https://mygmrs.com**),** or FRS: walkie-talkie radios. Explanation of each of these options will be discussed in this chapter.

Need for Communications: Communications is a critical part of any sheltering scenario. Not only is it critical to have communications between family members to coordinate the movements to and from shelters, it is essential to safety and emotional well-being to know where everyone is and how they are doing. Becoming separated in chaotic or threatening situations is not an acceptable option; therefore, communications is most critical. The effort to establish and maintain security is very difficult or impossible without reliable and effective communications. The need to deal with this need cannot be underestimated.

Consider CB, GMRS, FRS and/or HAM radio to keep in touch.
Do not rely entirely on cell phones.

Practice using radios effectively **BEFORE** the emergency. Two-way radio operation is not like using a telephone and requires practice. Otherwise, it will be very frustrating! Remember that everything you say on the air can be heard by anyone who wants to listen. Be careful what you say!

METHODS OF COMMUNICATIONS

CB Radio

The ease and low cost of CB (Citizens Band) mobile communications make this medium very attractive. There is no licensing requirement for the use of CB's, making them available for any "citizen" wishing to talk on them. *It is a very effective but also very non-secure means of short range communication.* With sophisticated antennas the range can be expanded for some distance. When conditions are right, "skip" can be experienced where the signal is sent great distances by bouncing off the ionosphere. However, this is an intermittent phenomenon and is not a reliable means for long range communications. The

CB radio has limited channel capacity and available channels will rapidly become overloaded in times of crises. Expect no more than a few miles of effective range depending on terrain.

Cell Phones

All cell towers are connected to land lines and they can be rendered ineffective by a variety of factors. For example, in New York, following the 9-11 attacks, intense cell phone traffic brought the communications system down, and those devices were thus unusable. Cell phone systems have limited capacity for traffic. "All circuits are busy. Please try your call later" can be heard during a normal day! Also be aware that in most localities, cell phone towers begin to shed parts when sustained winds reach around 80 mph (hurricanes, tornadoes). If telephone, land or microwave transmission is interrupted, cell service will also go down. It is important to have the important phone numbers written down on paper and carried with you. Having numbers stored in the cell phone may not do any good if the cell phone is not working.

Land based telephone line

Fewer and fewer land lines are being used these days. Many residences have eliminated stationary home phones altogether for the ease and portability of the cell phone. As a result, this transmission capacity is being reduced in order to divert resources to cell service. The reduced capacity of land lines may result in being unable to handle call demand. Again, the caller may hear: "All circuits are busy. Please try your call later". Pay phones are rare.

Radios

- **FRS**: "**Family Radio Service**" or "**walkie –talkies**" (shown above) are those you will see in parks, playgrounds and amusement parks. They are a very effective and reliable means of communications for parents to keep up with their kids or other groups. They are cheap and effective. However, they cannot be expected to operate beyond their purpose: very short range. Traditionally, they are considered "line of sight" radios. If you can see the other person, you can communicate with them. The range is usually between one half to one mile (despite whatever other claims are made) in a wooded or dense urban area, possibly more on open terrain. The claim of 2-5 miles may be true between two people on adjoining mountain peaks or on a prairie. No license is required for the use of these radios and they can be easily purchased in retail stores almost anywhere. Typically, these little radios transmit with ½ watt of power

EXAMPLE: Motorola
Talkabout MR350R

- **GMRS or "General Mobile Radio Service":** these radios use the same spectrum as the FRS radios and are limited to "line of sight" range. The main differences are that these radios <u>can</u> operate with higher power expanding the area of reception. <u>Also, the antennas can be detached and replaced by more efficient antennas which will provide increased range.</u> Remember that they are still a "short range" instrument. However, these radios are capable of utilizing a "repeater". A repeater is a separate device that receives the incoming signal, amplifies it and retransmits it on another frequency. This would allow one person to transmit on a GMRS radio to the repeater that may be mounted on the top of a building or mountain. The repeater would then retransmit that signal which could be received by another GMRS radio an equal distance away in the opposite direction. In simpler terms, one radio could talk to another radio 40 miles away if the repeater is between them. Terrain features could distort or shorten the "line of sight" signal.

NOTE: Using the GMRS radios and repeaters requires an FCC license. There are several good sites on the web that discuss the process; however, it is fairly informal and no testing is required. GMRS range can be significantly increased using repeaters but other options may provide greater flexibility.

- **HAM Radio:** The term "HAM" has no particular acronymic meaning, but was a nickname given in the early 20th century to amateur radio operators who liked to show off their capability by producing powerful radio interference to commercial radio stations. HAM today is a thriving international community of individuals connected by their love of the hobby. HAM amateur radio is divided into three categories: VHF (2 meters), UHF

(70 cm) and HF. The VHF or Very High Frequency and UHF or Ultra High Frequency is used also by police, fire and emergency services for direct communication. This communication medium is "line of sight".

HAM RADIO FACTORS AND LIMITATIONS:

- VHF or UHF HAM radio is generally effective over a distance up to 10-20 miles. Terrain, antenna, and transceiver power has a definite effect on both receiving and transmission. These radios are made in either mobile (vehicle mounted or hand held) or larger base stations. Operators are required to be licensed by the FCC (Federal Communications Commission). Many counties have clubs that provide support for its members for licensing and use of Ham radios.
- VHF and UHF repeaters are widely found across the United States and the world. Repeaters are often placed on high terrains and can cover entire regions. For example, one mobile radio could use a repeater fifty miles away and receive another radio 50 miles away in the opposite direction, making an effective range of 100 miles. Actual range varies with power, weather conditions, elevation, and natural or man- made obstructions.
- Repeaters can only receive and transmit one user at a time. There can be multiple users on the same repeater but as in any radio conversation, one person must be silent while another talks. In a time of crisis, these too will be over-run in traffic. Remember that there are many repeaters in many areas that can handle a lot of traffic, but like cell phones, in a time emergency the use of repeaters would likely not be effective for direct "one-on-one" communications with a loved one. However, this medium can be very effective to receive the flow of current information on "what's going on out there".
- Direct contact between HAM stations is known as simplex. This means that one ham operator speaks to another directly on a frequency outside of the "repeater" network. Again, as previously discussed, it is a "line of sight" situation. However, with a well planned VHF/UHF station, one could speak with a similar station many miles away. Simplex also means that when one party is transmitting; the other must listen until the transmission is complete before replying. **This communication is very much <u>unlike</u> <u>telephone </u> and requires practice before the operator can send and receive effectively.**

YAESU
VX-8GR
2M/440 5W HT BUILTIN GPS

The radio in the adjacent photo is commonly known as a "HT" or "handie-talkie". The real advantage of carrying this type of radio is that they can be very capable. It can transmit and receive on multiple bands. It can transmit and receive on VHF (2meter), (UHF) 440 (70cm) ham frequencies and also receive commercial FM and AM stations. It addition, it may receive, public service and NOAA (National Weather Service) transmissions. This would be very valuable in a time of emergency not only to communicate but to acquire situational awareness in the environment you are may be in. The one shown has a built in GPS. If you ever find yourself "bewildered" regarding your location in the turmoil of an emergency, you transmit your location on the same radio. These little radios can be a lifesaver. Beware however, they are low powered (5 watts) and have limited range.

HF: HIGH FREQUENCY OR (SHORT WAVE): is the best known medium where persons across the earth can communicate directly. This medium requires a properly configured antenna, radio, and FCC license. Signal strength is dependent on the quality and power of the radio transceiver, and the antennas both at transmitting and receiving site.

This signal is bounced off the ground, travels into space, and is bounced back to earth by the ionosphere where it is once again reflected into the upper atmosphere to be once more reflected. It is quite common for these signals to circle the earth as they bounce many times. This process is called *propagation* and allows the operators to conduct one-on-one communications at great distances. Most of the HF sets can be operated on DC (12 volts) current thus making them very portable.

Example Yaesu FT 897D

The radio shown above is one of the most capable ham radios on the market today. It has the capability of transmitting and receiving on **every** amateur band available: VHF, UHF and HF. It can serve as a base station or a mobile unit. It has the capability of an internal battery pack for portable power. It would be very suitable for the communication needs of the shelter and removed in a hurry if the need arises and taken off site or in a vehicle.

Ham radio offers the most communications independence and flexibility during a crisis, even if the operator is only listening to other transmissions.

NOTE: The FCC does require a license for the use of all Ham radios. Most every local area has a Ham radio club that offers testing and there are many effective study sites on the Web. HAMs are licensed at three levels: Technician, General, and Extra. The Technician level will grant all privileges for allotted UHF and VHF spectrum. High frequency (HF) utilization requires at least a General License.

REMINDER: all civilian radio transmissions can be heard by anyone having a receiver tuned to the appropriate frequency. Be VERY cautious about what information is spoken over the airwaves: there is no way to tell who might be listening.

Contact a local HAM club to discuss how to study for the required license or go on line to www.arrl.com

COMMUNICATIONS ADAPTATION

The previous material on Communications was taken from the companion volume entitled: **Evacuation: A Family Guide for the 21ˢᵗ Century.** Let's go through a few scenarios where communication is critical:

- Mobile security staff should always be in communication with all shelter stations.
- Staff within a shelter should be able to communicate internally and to adjacent shelters: Jump & run, short term and long term.
- Providing security zones in neighborhoods or individual structures.
- Between neighborhood check points and the command center.
  - **FRS or GMRS:** As previously described, are great little radios that will do fine so long as everything is short range.
  - **Ham Radio:** It is important that in each of the scenarios mentioned, you should have the same capability as mobile stations so that you can receive and transmit critical traffic. However, it is also important that the long term station have long range communication capability. This may be critical in asking for emergency medical evacuation or to simply know what is going on in the outside world. Knowing when help is coming and what you should do in the meantime is invaluable information.

⟹ *Study the chapter on Security regarding Neighborhoods.*

There is no real distinction in what is needed for one person or a community of people in the shelter. The only difference deals with the quantity of what is needed, so be prepared! Preparations should be made to maintain communications when the power goes out. If you have a radio mounted in your vehicle, you will hopefully have it in operating condition. If not, the battery should still be intact. Even if various automobiles are strewn about the place, there should be enough car batteries around to keep the radio supplied for a considerable amount of time.

As long as there is power left in a car battery, it can be used to provide power to various things, particularly Ham radios. Likewise, one can be used on an ongoing basis to provide backup power for a radio in full operation. Here is an image of a typical car battery permanently installed on the floor below the radio. If the power goes out a simple connection puts us back in business.

Of course, if you are using an HT, they will soon die without being recharged. Purchase a portable battery pack option now so you can use AA batteries if needed. A good supply of batteries in storage should keep you going for a while. To maintain the assurance of having an operating base station, care should be taken to assure it will survive the crisis. Having it in the safe room or in a shielded area would be preferable. Also, it can be moved to the safe area in haste if needed. Think in advance on how you would execute this process and be prepared to carry it out.

At most any quality auto supply store, you can purchase a small automatic battery charger. The one shown on the right is constantly plugged in and attached to the battery. If or when the power goes out , you can be assured that you will have a fully charged battery to power your radio. These little chargers are intended to maintain small batteries that usually sit idle for extended periods of time

such as boats or jet skis. They will charge the battery when needed and automatically shut off when the charge is complete. When the power goes off, you will have a fully charged battery that should supply the station for a considerable time. Of course the more batteries you have the longer the power will last.

In the above photo, three batteries are linked together and attached to a small "full time" battery charger. Each battery is rated at 90 amp hours. This means that each battery is capable of producing one amp of power for 90 hours. Using the formula covered in the electrical chapter: **watts/volts= amps** we can determine the following:

- The radio transmitting at full power is usually 50 watts

- Using the standard DC batteries (12 volts)

50/12 = 4.17 watts per hour

90 amp hour battery: 90/4.17= 21.59 hours

Therefore, a 90 amp hour battery will last over 21 ½ hours under full power.

Receiving (monitoring) power is obviously much less; usually between 3 to 4 watts. Using this scenario:

4/12=.34 watts per hour

90/.34=264 hours.

With the three of these linked together, the power supplied should be triple that (in theory).

Yaesu FT 897
Base/ Mobil Radio

AC Power Supply

Battery Charger

Here is the setup as described with a battery charger attached.. The radio is installed in a cabinet attached to the wall. It rest atop of a power source that converts normal house power: (AC 110 v) to DC. Even though the radio runs just fine this way, the battery charger remains attached to the battery located on the floor below the radio (previous photo shown). If power is ever lost, a simple connection to the battery is made and you are back in business with communications. Another real advantage to this arrangement is that the radio can be easily removed from the cabinet and relocated. The Yaesu FT 897 (shown) has a built in battery supply (optional) and would not need auxiliary power to operate. However, when the optional batteries are used to operate the radio, the power goes from 100 watt output to 35 watts.

Yaesu FT 8800 Mobile Radio

Mobile Communications can be used for stationary operations. The vehicle simply becomes the base of operations for communications. This is both an advantage and a disadvantage. As stated previously, the battery simply needs to be intact to provide power and you will have communications. However, it is attached to the car. In the case of a tornado, the car can be tossed somewhere else and damage the radio. A flood, of course, will destroy both the car and the radio. If preparation is made in advance, the mobile radio can be easily removed from the car, taken to the shelter, attached to a battery and serve its intended purpose. Remember however, in the event that the radio is removed from the car another antenna would need to be attached.

Antennas can be very easily made using common materials. This is a subject to itself which could take much more space than intended by this text. However, you will find the plans for a simple "j-pole" antenna made from copper pipe commonly found at home improvement or hardware stores on line free of charge. In your search engine, simply type: J pole antenna. You should get all the instructions that you need. This antenna could easily be hung from a rafter in the attic or at any place inside or outside and will work for all 2 meter (VHF) frequencies. Plan in advance how you could make a mobile unit work in a stationary environment.

The **mobile antenna will work just fine** mounted on a kitchen table; just be sure that you have all of the connections necessary to make the conversion.

EMERGENCY RADIO COMMUNICATIONS: WHEN AND WHERE?

The discussion of ham radio bands and frequencies is a very big subject that would take extensive time and space to cover and beyond the scope of this book. Suffice it to say that the use of the airwaves for amateur radio is granted by the FCC (Federal Communications Commission) and includes several *bands*. Within each of these bands there are a series of *frequencies*. These bands are identified by the *wavelength* of the radio signal and the *frequency* refers to the speed of the radio wave. Each of these bands behaves differently depending on condition of the atmosphere. They can change with climate, seasons, day, night time and the behavior of the sun. As a result, it becomes ill-advised to make broad suggestions on when and where to use specific ham bands to communicate with a chosen station at any given point in time.

Ham radio is a method of communication using no infrastructure. This is the reason it is the method of choice in emergency situations. It is also the biggest challenge when you expect it to perform just like a telephone where you can

74

pick it up at any time and dial the number of the person you want to communicate with.

This is especially true for HF (high frequency) long range communications. Atmospheric conditions would most likely be different in your part of the world than the station you choose to speak with. In any event, when it comes to ham radio, time zones are very small. When a person one continent speaks to a person on another, they are most certainly experiencing different parts of the day or in another day entirely. This is one time where you can actually speak with *yesterday* and to *tomorrow* at the same time.

As a result, you will need to become familiar with the behavior of the different ham radio bands. One easy way of doing this is to go on line and type: **Propagation Prediction Program.** These programs are free and at any given time, can determine the current conditions of the various components in the atmosphere, at both points of interest, and tell you the best ham band to use. Of course, the use of this program is dependent on having a working computer which may not be the case. After a while, you will be able to make some judgments regarding rough consistencies in the information it has provided. As a result, you should be able to make an outline for times and locations with your long distance friends. It is recommended that you establish times to communicate with them on a regular basis before a crisis. It is very common to hear friends speaking with each other across the country on 80 meters every single day. This way you will know in advance how the conditions behave and during times of emergency you can continue with your normal practices.

In times of emergency the VHF and UHF frequencies will experience a great deal of traffic. Amateur radio clubs are established across the country and many are dedicated to the purpose of providing emergency radio communications in times of emergency. Within these clubs is a program called **ARES (Amateur Radio Emergency Service) or RACES (Radio Amateur Civil Emergency Service).** Information on these can be located at: www.arrl.org/ares, or www.usraces.org.
In most cases, each of these clubs has trustees (owners/caretakers) of repeaters as their members. They will dedicate these repeaters in times of emergency to serve the community. The traffic (communication) is prioritized in the following order:

- **EMERGENCY**—Any message having life and death urgency to any person or group of persons, that is transmitted by Amateur Radio in the absence of regular commercial facilities. This includes official messages of welfare agencies during emergencies requesting supplies, materials or instructions vital to relief efforts for the stricken populace in emergency areas. On CW

(Morse code) and digital modes, this designation will always be spelled out. *When in doubt, do not use this designation.*

- **PRIORITY**—Abbreviated as P on CW and digital modes. This classification is for important messages having a specific time limit, official messages not covered in the emergency category, press dispatches and emergency-related traffic not of the utmost urgency.
- **WELFARE**—Abbreviated as W on CW and digital modes. This classification refers to an inquiry about the health and welfare of an individual in the disaster area, or to an advisory from the disaster area that indicates all is well. Welfare traffic is handled only after all Emergency and Priority traffic is cleared. The Red Cross equivalent to an incoming Welfare message is DWI (Disaster Welfare Inquiry).
- **ROUTINE**— Abbreviated as R on CW and digital modes. Most traffic in normal times will bear this designation. In disaster situations, traffic labeled Routine should be handled last, or not at all when circuits are busy with higher-precedence traffic.[6]

GET INVOLVED

The folks you will find on the radio during these times are members of these groups are dedicated to service and would be a great asset for you and your family in times of need. We encourage you to be familiar with your local group and how to monitor their repeater. Of course, better still is to become a member of one of these groups. You will always be on the leading edge of emergency information and be in a great position to serve yourself, you family and community. Also, by being a member of one of these groups you will get to know the local liaison to the group. This is usually an emergency management administrator (EMA) that has ties with all of the emergency service facilities in the county. You will also be able to participate with them on emergency drills that they have from time to time and rub shoulders with the police and fireman in your area. This too would be a great asset in times of need.

- **CERT (Community Emergency Response Teams):**

In addition, we recommend that you consider **CERT (Community Emergency Response Teams)** training that may be available in your area. You can gather information on this on line. Courses may be available in your area which would

---

[6] http://www.arrl.org/files/file/ARESFieldResourcesManual.pdf

again, help you become familiar with the local emergency staff. In many cases the training will be located in local police and fire stations where you will get to know your local law enforcement and fire fighting personnel personally.

- **ARES: Amateur Radio Emergency Services)**

Check out: www.arrl.org and take the online courses on emergency communication. Courses EC-001 (Introduction to Amateur Radio Emergency Communications) Level 1 and EC-002 (Intermediate Amateur Radio Emergency Communications) Level II would be great training and help you understand the traffic being made during these times.

In times of emergency, ham radio repeaters will be tied up with emergency traffic by those in one of these groups. If you become involved in the group, you will have direct access to the repeater in connection with your responsibility. This will translate to a greater ability to do what you need to do to transmit and receive emergency traffic that can have a direct impact on your situation. Get involved! As you help others, you will be able to better help yourself.

- **There will be no better source of emergency information anywhere on the airwaves than from your local Ham radio neighbors.**

In absence of this possibility, establish a *simplex* frequency that you can establish communication with friends and family. Also, establish times that you will be monitoring. Listen to what is going on and transmit only when you have something to say. Chances are the local EMA (Emergency Management Agency) will be equipped and monitoring the VHF and/or UHF frequencies without interruption. If necessary, they can serve as "relays" between one station and another, especially if it is emergency traffic. Find out in advance what band and frequency they will be monitoring. This information should be available through the local ARES or RACES groups. In an effort to save precious battery life, you may not want to leave the radio on all of the time. Depending on the severity of the emergency, you may want to monitor on hourly intervals.

Here is a simple chart that may help you get started in the right direction:

Day	Time	Band	Frequency Primary	Frequency Secondary

Summary: The FRS radios are cheap and effective. However, they only put out ½ watt and have very short range. The GMRS radios are better as they can generate more power and have "repeater" capability. Hand held Ham radios, usually generate 5 watts and also have "repeater capability". Mobile Ham radio stations typically generate between 50 and 75 watts and have multiple antenna options giving it tremendous power and capability. Mobile HF is very viable but expensive and temperamental.

Base station HF will generate the best long distance communication system anywhere. Another option is to find a surplus commercial or public safety radio that can be programmed to the ham band such as a Motorola Saber. They typically generate 5 watts.

Get licensed in Ham radio and get involved. Join the local radio club and emergency service groups. Look into CERT training and involve the entire family in the exercise. This will help you develop a mentality of emergency preparedness that will greatly assist you in the effort to protect your family in times of need.

Chapter 8

WHERE TO SHELTER

Tent as a temporary shelter in Oklahoma (ID: 44331) Shawnee, OK, May 13, 2010 -- A tent provides homeowners with temporary shelter following the destruction of their home by an F3 tornado. A series of 22 confirmed tornadoes swept across central and eastern Oklahoma on Monday, May 10th. FEMA Photo by Win Henderson

This may seem like a pretty silly question (where to shelter) if your intent is to stay with your stuff and to protect it from the bad guys. However, the primary concern should be to live through the experience in the process. There is no amount of property that is worth your life. The question then becomes, "can I provide a secure area around my stuff and be in a position where I can protect myself and my family? If the answer is yes, then we are good to go.

⇨ *Study the chapter on Security*

In the worst case scenario, there is local or regional chaos. You are not the only one looking for a secure environment, a safe place to stay and to be among friends. In many cases your friends will see you as the one to be with if things really get bad. Are you ready? Do you have sufficient supplies to provide for them or are you going to turn them away? What if they are family? Does this change the security scenario? Can you provide security for yourself, your family and all of those who show up at your door-step wanting you to help them?

Consider in advance what you will do and where you will go. If yours is the place to be, let those know who are welcome and who are not. **Have the supplies and resources in place in advance to accommodate them!** If they show up unannounced, let them know that they need to come with sufficient supplies to provide for themselves. If you cannot turn them away, YOU need to plan in advance to provide for them.

⇨ *Study the Chapters on Food and Water.*

Depending on how many you are anticipating, you will need to consider what *type of facility* yours will fall into. These facilities are described in the following pages. An area may be secure for a small number of people but not so much for a larger number. It is a bad situation to be in to have your plan all in place, be ready for the event to occur and find yourself overwhelmed when others show up wanting your help.

Determine in advance, where you will go and what supplies you will have there. Make sure that those you love know where they are expected to go and that they know what they should do. Have a written plan and review it often with them.

⇨ *See the Checklist & Reference Section.* Things may change from time to time that will necessitate adjustments to the plan. Keep it current and distributed as needed.

TYPES OF FACILITIES

(Sheltering in Place facilities falls into three main categories)

"Jump and Run"

This title has reference to "hot" landing zones. The military choppers would lower within feet of the ground for the troops to jump off and run for cover. It is not a safe place to be. It is just a location for drop off and pickup which is necessary because of the circumstances. It may also serve as a location where you would want to stop along the way toward your ultimate shelter location.

Similar circumstances may arise in your personal situation. This is more of a rally point than a place to stay. However, there will be places that people (relatives and friends) accumulate looking for help. They may come to a friend's house. The problem is that the house is located in a volatile area that is not possible to provide security. They may assemble there but it is not wise to stay very long. There is little to no working facilities here. There may be no sanitation or cooking facilities here. It may be in an area prone to violence.

Hopefully, no more than a few moments should be taken to receive supplies, instructions, directions and to get them on their way. Transportation may need to be provided by friends or relatives to move them to a short or long term site. Jump and run means: "Good to see you; Glad you made it. Now, here is where you need to go and here is how you need to get there…..go!" It is implied that someone may need to be positioned there to receive and transfer the arrivals.

Pre-determined times and places can be arranged in advance to avoid the constant staffing of this location. If staffing is necessary, this person should be sufficiently trained on scenario options, how to proceed with each option and have the ability to execute the plan. Another option is to have materials and supplies pre-staged there with instructions on how to proceed to the next stage of sheltering. An overnight stay at this location would be risky and should be avoided. Remember, adequate security cannot be provided in these locations.

Short Term

These locations are intended to accommodate refugees for up to three days. In these cases, the security may be better than the "jump and run" but not much better. Some short term security can be provided but there are limited supplies here. The reason there are limited supplies here is because they cannot be secured. As you can see, without the ability to provide security you have no absence of fear and doubt. However, we improvise and do the best that we can do and in some cases, this is all that we can do and that is OK.

In these locations, everyone would need to jump in and be involved in every aspect of the situation. There are not enough people there to have anyone not contributing unless they are injured or sick. Security watches would need to be rotated among reliable personnel for 24-7 surveillance of the entire facility including perimeters. Short range communications should be present here so that the long term facility knows what supplies are needed and how many people need to be transferred there.

Long Term

When sheltering in place, this is the "destination". This is a facility where sufficient supplies are on hand to accommodate all present (or at least all that the supplies that we have). There is security in place here to protect the supplies and the occupants. This is where we are going to hang out until the crisis is over. Cooking, sanitation and sleeping facilities are available. Hopefully, reliable short and long range communication is here as well.

These three categories can be adapted to an individual or to a community. It just needs to developed and reviewed as needed.

Chapter 9

GETTING AROUND

Plaquemines Parish, LA, 9/21/2005 -- A freezer truck containing fish is left leaning against a tree in the front yard of a destroyed residence in Plaquemines Parish. FEMA photo/Andrea Booher

TRANSPORTATION
(How do I get around?)

In most cases transportation during emergency situations is done on an "as needed" basis and can be difficult. During severe storm scenarios where the whole place is torn up, private vehicles and public transportation systems were not spared the wrath. Sheltering in place usually means just that: staying put. Transportation then becomes necessary for reasons of security such as the need to vacate the shelter under threat of harm or to rescue someone else from pending danger in a "jump & run" location. ⟹ **Study the chapter on Where to shelter.**

In any event, no vehicle will be effective without fuel. Remember that survival is a mindset as much as it is anything else. Have ample fuel storage on hand in case it becomes unavailable and where it is safe. Typically, gas stations receive resupply on a very regular basis. If the trucks can't move as a result of the emergency, this supply will leave them very empty very fast. Of course, this is a inevitable if commercial power is interrupted. It takes power to run the pumps, no power, no gas. The most reasonable solution is to plan on several methods, motorized, mechanical or by foot if necessary. Be prepared to execute whatever plan for transportation is needed.

If you have a location where you can keep some extra fuel, it would be a good idea to do so. At least have enough for one replacement tank. Just be sure to rotate. Gasoline will spoil fairly quickly: six months to a year. Diesel fuel will store much longer.

Alternative means of transportation

Of course, when we think of transportation, we will automatically think of automobiles in all of their varieties. They will give us the greatest degree of speed and safety but may not necessarily be the best way to get around in a crisis. In the case of large scale storms, the area is strewn with debris, everywhere. Roads are impassable. It may take days to clear them with chainsaws and heavy equipment. If you live in a more rural area it may take much longer. It may be up to you to clear the road. This is presuming that there is a home (something) to get to in the first place.

Alternative means of transportation can include utility vehicles such as golf carts, all terrain vehicles (ATV), motorcycles, bicycles, farm tractors and even lawn mowers. Whatever will move can become a viable alternative to walking.

Of course, if you have the means, equine have served the purpose of carrying man for longer than anything else we know of except maybe camels!

Should I move around?

The matter of having transportation and using it is two different issues to consider. It is often the case that it would be better to be stationary in the event of an emergency or crisis rather than exposing yourself or your vehicle to those around you. It is important that you study the chapter on Security and specifically the subject of moment contained therein. Particularly in the case of riot or mob activity it; would be unwise to travel near that event. ⟹ *(Study the chapter on Security: Personal movement during a secure situation).*

EMP

There is much concern recently, regarding the potential damage to electronic components caused by an Electromagnetic Pulse (EMP). It is basically a burst of Electromagnetic radiation that provides damaging current. This current could disrupt or destroy electronic components of all types. With most modern forms of transportation heavily invested in electronic technology, this event could render a severe blow to our ability to get around. This is an event that would have far reaching implications and would require major independent research and preparation.

The electronic devises contained in vehicles and other means of transportation can be protected with the right preparation. Study the subject of **Faraday Cages** on line or in your local library.

Note:

One of the simplest thing you can do is to make sure that you have plenty of gas in the car at all times. Make it a habit to fill up when the tank reaches ½. It is often the case that the actual vehicle is in fine shape, it just does not have any fuel and the gas stations are all closed. Make an effort that this does not happen to you. Also, if you are serious about preparing for emergency situations, it would be advisable to invest in a four wheel drive vehicle. If it is a truck type, install a winch on the front and keep emergency supplies on board in case they are needed.

Chapter 10

INSURANCE

Home demolished by the tornado of April 2011, north of Anniston , Ala

Many times when you decide to shelter in place and ride out the storm, things work out ok. Sometimes they don't. In some cases you miraculously survived the storm with your life, but your home did not fare so well. Now what? Hopefully, you had insurance. If not, there may be governmental or charitable agencies offering assistance.

The subject of insurance in the context of our discussion is varied. Coverages and Insurance Providers vary greatly by state. Our purpose here is to outline a few basic principles that may be similar in the American market place. We will put a very small bit of information in your hands that may assist as you consider what you need to do.

If you live in an area subject to storms, like those on the Gulf Coast, there is a good chance that the number of insurance providers available to purchase property insurance from is limited. There is a good reason for that and it is important that you understand why. In order to do that, a little background needs to be laid first.

TYPES OF INSURANCE PROVIDERS

There are thousands of different insurance carriers operating in the United States. Some only operate in one state or in one region. There are some carriers that operate in every state. Usually, these are going to be names well recognized by most of you. In most cases, they are part of larger organizations that are involved in other parts of the financial sectors of the economy and have assets around the world.

If their base of operation is located (Domiciled) in the state where you live, they are considered a **Domestic** Carrier. If it is located in another state but still within the United States it is considered **Foreign.** If they are domicile in another country, they are considered **Alien.**

The Insurance Industry is probably the most regulated industry in existence. Each of these carriers has to operate within the laws set by each state in which they operate. Regulations vary from state to state. Carriers are allowed to do different things in different states as governed by the State Department of Insurance. It is overseen by the Insurance Commissioner.

Insurance carriers are regulated on what coverages they can provide and what rates they can charge. Their coverage forms need approval and will be highly scrutinized in most cases. These are the carriers that are allowed to solicit for the best rated insurance customers in the area. These insurance carriers will usually provide the best rates and the best coverage. These are also the carriers that are considered **Admitted**. Admitted carriers must comply with all of the regulations relating to pricing and coverage as well as participate in the "insolvency pool". They are charged their "share" of this pool by the regulators.

If an Insurance Carrier becomes unable to pay the claims it is presented with due to catastrophic losses or various other reasons, the Admitted carriers in the state are accessed their share of the losses. This is the purpose of the "insolvency pool" to protect the insurance consumer from insolvent insurance providers.

Insurance providers who choose to write the business associated with higher risk can be allowed to operate in the state on a **"non-admitted"** basis. They write the business not written by the admitted carriers who are not allowed to charge more than the rates they have had approved by the regulators. Thus, this is called **"surplus lines"** of insurance. This will be discussed further in the following section.

If the assessments from this insolvency pool become burdensome or if the insurance regulators in the state do not approve the carriers request to increase their rates to cover their losses, they will withdraw from the state entirely. In those cases, the non-admitted carriers writing the non standard or surplus lines business will become a major player.

TYPES OF INSURANCE BUSINESS

In an effort to help the consumer have access to all types of insurance, the regulators in each state insurance department realize an additional need exists. In order to qualify for the *admitted* carriers who have the best coverages and cheapest rates, the insurance consumer must have a good loss ratio and offer the potential for the insurance carrier to make a profit. They solicit the *standard business*, the cream of the crop.

There will many consumers who will not qualify for the "standard market place" for various reasons. In many states the option to purchase automobile insurance is not an option; it is required by law. So, in an effort to meet the needs of those in these situations, the regulators allow other carriers to operate in the state on a *surplus lines* basis. That is to take up the slack where the "admitted carriers" will not write them.

These carriers are called **Non Admitted** Carriers, writing *surplus lines* of insurance. They are allowed to charge higher rates and have differences in coverage forms. They solicit the **"Non- Standard Business"**: that business that is rejected by the Standard Carriers.

Generally speaking, the best rates and coverages will be provided by the admitted carriers who write the standard business.

METHOD OF PURCHASING

Now, to further the discussion, it is important to understand that all carriers fall in two main categories: Direct Writers and Agent based. This refers to their method in soliciting business.

o **Direct writers** are those you will see on TV with all of the fancy mascots and clever commercials prompting you to call them direct and to "cut out the middle man". In these cases, you are dealing directly with the insurance provider itself. They will sell you **their** product directly. Other examples of these are those carriers who have neighborhood agents who can only write for one carrier.

o The **Agent Based Carriers** are those who choose to use independent agents as a source of their business. The agent will take the information from the customer, prepare the necessary paperwork and submit it to the appropriate insurance carrier for policy issuance.

The reason that this is explained is that it can make a big difference on the types of coverage provided. For example, a "Direct Writer" insurance provider will issue their policies on "*manuscript*" paper. In other words, it is proprietary to them alone. They determine what is covered and what is not and the "coverage form" is not found in the inventory of its competitors.

POLICY COVERAGE FORMS

There is no strict uniformity among the policy documents between Direct Writers. That is not to say that the coverages are not similar because they are; it is just that the exact working can vary and be subject to conflicting legal interpretation according to their own loss experience and will be written to favor them.

The carriers described as "Agent Based" will usually have uniformity in policy forms. The Insurance Services Office (ISO) is a non-profit organization funded by all participating insurance carriers to create and maintain uniform insurance documents. They are widely used across the United States. These carriers will use these coverage forms to construct their policies. One coverage document will be identical to the coverage document used by a competing carrier. The competitive differences are the pricing and elected coverage provided from these forms.

Policy forms are basically written on two types: Named Peril or Special.

- **Named Peril** policy forms will start off with a few basic coverages and exclude the rest. You can then go back and add the coverage you want thus explaining the term: "named peril". In other words, everything is excluded unless it is named as a covered peril. **Special attention should be paid as to what is covered.**

- **Special** policy forms are just about the opposite of Named Peril. In this case, everything is covered unless it is excluded. **Special attention should be paid to what is excluded.**

In the context of our concern with catastrophic losses, most property insurance claims you will face should be covered with a quality homeowner insurance policy. For example, the major hazards associated with catastrophic events are fire, lightning, windstorm, hail, smoke, falling objects, weight of ice or snow and freezing are covered on the basic named peril (HO3) policy form issued by the ISO.

There are two glaring exceptions to this general rule. If you live in an area where there is a "known hazard" and presents an exceptional loss potential to the insurance carrier, they may elect to exclude these specific perils to protect them from catastrophic financial loss.

These two perils are specifically wind and flood. It is important that you actually read your policy and study the Conditions, Endorsement and Exclusion forms.

TYPES OF COVERAGE

- **Property**
  - ## Wind

If you live on or near the beaches of the Gulf of Mexico, you will be able to buy a homeowner policy but it will usually exclude the perils of wind and flood. Coverages for these perils will have to be purchased on their own and will most likely cost as much or more than the primary coverage depending on what flood zone you are located in. It is important that you speak with your insurance representative to determine exactly where you stand on this issue.

  - ## Flood

This has been the subject for many courtrooms, following the hurricanes on the Gulf Coast of the United States. As mentioned before, flood insurance will most likely be excluded from any primary insurance coverage provided for a property is in a known flood zone. The coverage for this can be very, very expensive. As a result, many residences will simply take their chances and hope for the best. Besides, it is in a 100 year flood plain right? What are the chances it will happen in my lifetime? I think I will save that money and have an extra barbeque this year. Well, it seems that fate always has a way of dealing with us harshly. We may soon be on our roof with a white hankie waving it frantically at the Coast Guard Choppers hovering nearby and looking for a ride.

Also, be aware that according to your insurance coverage documents there is a big difference between wind driven rain and flood.

Wind driven rain is exactly that: moisture that falls from the sky and is forced into areas such as homes and structures by the wind. If this happens long enough, it will most likely cause the place to look like it has been flooded but was not a flood by definition.

Flood water is water that rises from the earth either by tides, waves or surges. It carries with it, all that rest on the water such as debris and contaminates. It does not necessarily become airborne.

In an effort to appease the plight of many of those who did not have flood insurance and partitioned the government for help, many courts have ruled against the insurance carriers and have forced them to pay for excluded flood damages even though flood was not the culprit, it was wind driven rain. Some insurance carriers have been put out of business for having to pay for flood losses they never collected premiums for. In any event, it is important that you know the difference and be prepared, to do the right thing so that you will have what you need when the times comes.

- ○ **Earth Movement**

Otherwise known as Earthquake, will usually be excluded. Separate Earthquake policies may be purchased.

- ○ **Nuclear, Government action and acts of War will most always be excluded.**

There is little to no alternative coverage available for these perils in the Standard market place.

- • **Automobile**

In contrast to the discussion on the property, the subject of Automobile insurance is quite simple. Automobile insurance is divided into two main categories: Liability and Physical Damage.

- ○ **Liability** protects you against any legal liability you may occur as a result of your action while driving an automobile: you hit someone and damage them and/ or their property.

- ○ **Physical Damage** is coverage intended to protect you against damage sustained to your vehicle. This is divided into two main categories:

  - ▪ **Comprehensive:** This usually covers the vehicle while it is stationary. A tree falling on it, being tossed around by a tornado or floating away in the flood. In most cases this is the coverage that will apply to the situations we are discussing unless you are operating it at the time.

  - ▪ **Collision:** you accidently run into a tree or someone else and damage your car.

There will usually be deductibles associated with the physical damage coverage.

TERRORISM

This is an interesting subject for discussion and the origin for an evolution of insurance coverage in the United States. Prior to the attacks on September 11, 2001, acts of war (including terrorism) were excluded from most all domestic insurance policies. There is simply no way for the insurance carrier to financially plan for such an event and certainly no way to build the appropriate rates into the premium to survive such an event. However, amidst the national outcry and outrage following 9-11, it would be politically unwise for any carrier to announce on the national news that it would not respond to the claims they would be presenting.

As a result, Terrorism coverage has been built into most commercial policies since then, with the option to exclude it. This exclusion would have to be in writing by endorsement. **Depending on the state in which you reside, Terrorism may or may not be included in your personal insurance property policies.** Read your policy or check with your insurance representative to determine you specific circumstance.

Summary

Knowing where you stand with these carriers and who will stand behind your claim will go a long way toward your recovery. Use this knowledge well in advance of the crisis to put your insurance purchases in the right places.

Know what your coverages are and be prepared to exercise the right ot claim on them when the times comes. Copies of all of your insurance policies along with contact names and numbers should be in a secured area that will not be destroyed by the crisis. Consider placing them in a secured box in your safe room or off site where they will be secured and easily retrieved if needed.

As you look at the tattered residence that was once your home, you need to rest assured that you will be able to recover financially (at least) from the trauma you have endured. By understanding the basic principles outlined above you should be able to get a better understanding on what type of coverage you have and what kinds you need.

SCENARIOS

So far, we have pointed out some of the concerns you may face in the case of emergency. You have a busy life and little time set aside for these things. Besides, it is something that *may* happen in the future, maybe a long time in the future. "I will deal with it when the times come" is a common thought.

Each situation is unique and presents its own challenges. To prepare for each, takes training specific to the event. In the following sections, you will find emergency situations (scenarios) that have been outlined in detail. These are the typical situations that you may face when having to make the decision to shelter at home. Study them and take whatever information you can to apply to your specific situation. Use them as a resource to accomplish your goal.

Chapter 11

TORNADO

Joplin, MO, May 24, 2011 -- Homes were leveled with the force of 200 mph winds as a F5 tornado struck the city the night of May 22, 2011. FEMA is coordinating the effort to help the survivors and the community. Jace Anderson/FEMA

In none of the recovery situations I have participated in has the awesome power of Mother Nature been more on display than by this scenario. It is hard to run from a tornado because its path is unpredictable. In this scenario prior planning is key to survival. Have a safe place to go that is VERY nearby. This is critical and may make the difference between life and death. If you have ever witnessed this devastation, you may wonder if there is any way to survive its awesome power. Truly, if you are in its path and it has "set down" on the surface of the earth, there will be nothing standing behind it. Being below ground may be the only option; and even then, preparation must be made to survive its fury.

Structures built on concrete slabs poured directly on the earth (slab on grade) present the greatest challenges for protection. There are countless stories of those who have survived doing various things such as lying down in a bathtub and covering up with a mattress or some other protective object. Others have survived hiding in an interior room, closet or bathroom. Again, under the same situations, others who have practiced the exact same techniques have perished. You simply cannot tell in advance what the winds will do exactly until it is too late.

The only way to exercise the most proven means of survival is to be below ground level. Safe rooms are being utilized more and more often for personal protection against hazards of many types. With a little forethought and determination, they can be built effectively and economically.

The Federal Emergency Management Association (FEMA) has many such plans for carrying out such a task. A few simple examples follow. Each of these can be found on their web site: www.FEMA.gov.

SAFE ROOMS

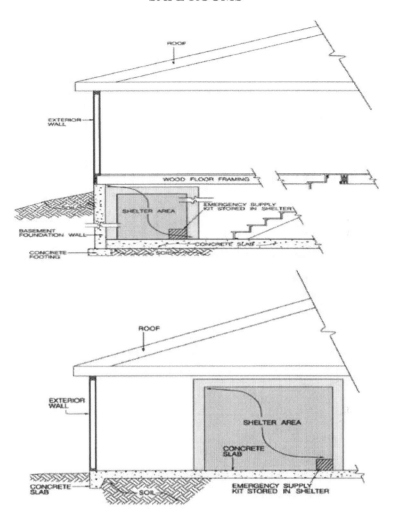

The previous images will give you a general understanding of what is intended with the safe room. It is a room built away from the exterior walls near the center of the home. The walls, ceilings and floor are reinforced and anchored to each other. Emergency supplies are stored in the room in case you have to get in there in a hurry and have to time to assemble them.

Very detailed plans are available from the FEMA web site. Below you can see a few examples. Here is one for a basement Lean-to.

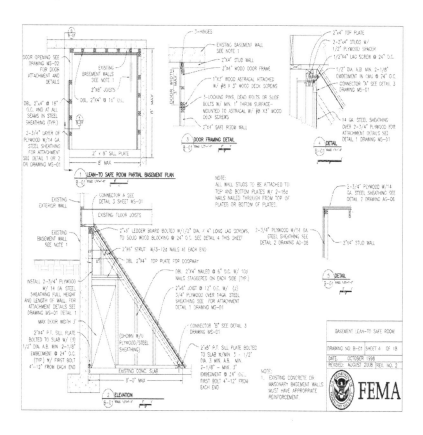

Another alternative is in the corner of the basement. The room has its own ceiling (below the floor joists above) with hardened walls and entry. As you can see, there are no sharp edges, nothing that will catch the wind. It is streamlined and should survive just fine if it is properly anchored to the walls and floor.

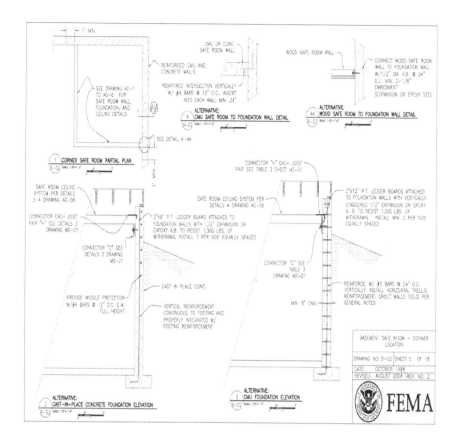

Safe rooms do not have to be expensive. Most of our homes today were not built with a safe room in mind. Even in a fully constructed home, however, it is not too late to make a room that will be much stronger than the remainder of the home. In the process of retrofitting this room, you will most likely make a mess of the house for a while. But that is OK. Just stay on task and get the job done.
.

Safe Rooms can be independent structures away from the home, maybe in a back yard. This is an in ground structure with separate ventilation, also courtesy of FEMA.

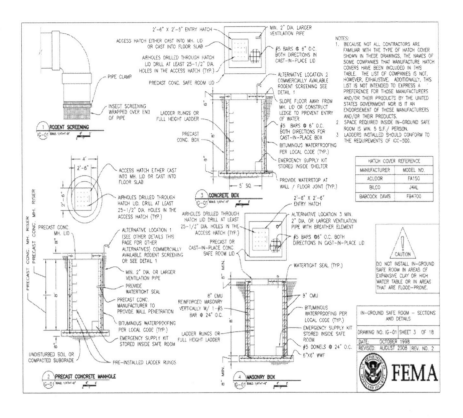

The following illustration gives direction on how you can take an existing room (in this case a bathroom) in the house and make it double as a safe room.

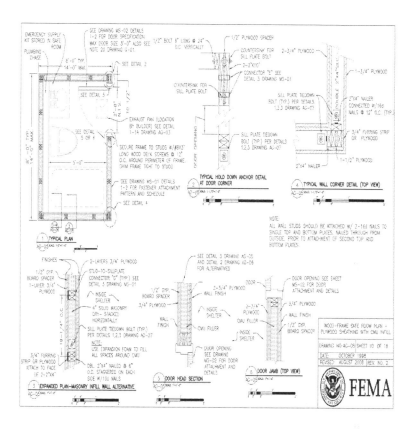

- Consider constructing a room into which you can retreat from a storm or intruders and await reinforcements or rescue when other security measures have failed. This will be a hardened or safe room.
- Remember however, that a storm safe room and a safe room for security purposes may differ in details.
- The walls would need to be extra sturdy, with steel studs and very small (if any) space between studs so tearing external drywall away would not allow entrance or even access to the space. Door frames would be reinforced and extra lock installed.
- A small cache of appropriate supplies should be positioned inside the room.
- The room should be ventilated in a manner that intruders would not be able to readily discover.

o   Locate basic emergency supplies in the safe room. Consider storing a few tools such as a hammer, crowbar, hack saw and wood hand saw.

o   You may also choose to make the room fire resistant. Discuss that with a contractor. Fire is possibly the most dangerous threat to safe room occupants. In addition to having an extinguisher in the safe room; consider placing another on your path to the exit. Teach the children how to use them. Extinguishers can also repel or detract intruders.

ENTRAPMENT

One of the greatest concerns with a tornado is entrapment. You have survived the storm but what is left of the structure has been reduced to rubble and piled on top of you. You are now at the mercy of the first responders, friends and neighbors to find and rescue you. This may take a while! Hopefully no more than a few hours but sometimes it may take several days.

The same storm system that produced the deadly tornado which hit Joplin, Missouri in May 2011, produced bad weather for several days following the storm. This hampered rescue efforts as another tornado warning was issued for the city that following evening. The rescue personnel were themselves evacuated.

⇨   *(Study the chapter on Medical regarding issues associated with entrapment).*

When considering where to build your safe room, think about what would happen under these circumstances. Could you get out of your safe room? How hard would it be for the rescuers to find you? Could they hear your cries for help? How long do you think that your voice would hold up under these circumstances, constantly yelling for help?

An alternative means for "making noise" would be good. Have a whistle readily accessible in the shelter. With a little effort, you can make a lot of noise. Better still is to have a safe room where the exit would not be easily obstructed.

Self contained shelters previously shown are best for this purpose. Of course, that means that you have to leave your home to enter the shelter. You may get wet and blown around a bit before you can get in, but it is a good and viable option.

Consider that you have been protected from the storm; you are underground in a safe room and the storm removed your house, reduced it to its base components and randomly distributed it (along with many others) within a five square mile radius. **What other things would you like to have in the shelter with you?**

⟹ **(See the Checklist and Reference Material section on Good things to have around the shelter and *72 hour kit assembly).**

Where are your important papers such as titles, deeds, birth, marriage and stock certificates? Indeed, you are happy that you survived but with a little bit more effort you can make your life following the storm less hectic. You should have sufficient supplies to sustain yourself for a while in case of entrapment.

Signaling the outside world
- o Escape from entrapment may require signaling rescuers. If activity is heard outside, signaling should begin immediately.
- o Voice (calling or screaming) **is not effective** and will only wear out the voice and increase anxiety among the entrapped.
- o Keep whistles and a hammer or pieces of metal (1" diameter reinforcing bar, 1 ft. long) in the room. These can be used to repeatedly strike wood or metal inside the wreckage. Steady knocking noises are often more easily heard by rescuers than voices. Taps, whistles or knocking from within wreckage will likely be noticed by anyone near your position.
- o Having a GMRS/FRS radio with batteries in your shelter kit, would make it much easier to contact someone on the outside. The best radio to have would be one that has a scan function that could be turned on and would thus enable you to pick up a signal and converse if anyone in the area was transmitting. These radios are inexpensive and commonly used by civilians for outdoor activities and recreation.

Note: if you are able to communicate in any way with would be rescuers, your chances of being high on the rescue list are greatly improved.

For a full download on how a safe room can be built, see:
http://www.fema.gov/plan/prevent/saferoom/shplans/

Above Photo: Here is an example of a low cost shelter. A family north of Anniston, Alabama survived the devastating tornado of April 2010 that destroyed their home by hiding in this cargo van buried in the hillside.

Chapter 12

HURRICANE

Biloxi, Miss., November 3, 2005 -- The Hwy 90 Bridge from Biloxi to Ocean Springs lies in a twisted mass as result of catastrophic wind and storm surge from Hurricane Katrina. Road closure along the coastal area has complicated recovery efforts. George Armstrong/FEMA

Having lived and/or worked on the gulf coast of the United States since the late 1970's I have had my share of hurricane experiences. I had to evacuate many times and sometimes twice in the same season. Residents of the area are all too familiar with the drill.

In most cases the storms are taken in stride; the leaves and debris are cleaned up and within a few days and life goes back to normal. It is only in the rare event of Category 5 storms making landfall in your yard that life on the beach is reevaluated by many. In these cases, jobs, homes and lives are lost. It is truly nature's fury in its greatest display. As a result, these storms are not to be taken lightly. Our advice is to listen to the local authorities. If they tell you that you should leave, then that is exactly what you should do.

According to USGS, 50% of the US population lives within 50 miles of the coast. A hurricane could strike anywhere from the Gulf Coast to New England. If you live in these areas, you need a thorough understanding of the threat, and a good plan. Tsunami risk is higher in many nations bordering the Pacific, and while these events are not frequent, they can be catastrophic in scope and duration.

The two catastrophic events associated with Hurricane is windstorm and flooding.

- *Windstorm*

⇨ *(Study the Chapters onTornado)*

Inland from the beach, windstorm is the primary hazard associated with a Hurricane. Sheltering in the path of the storm is survivable so far as the wind is concerned.

- **Flooding**

⇨ *(Study the Chapter: When Evacuation is the only option)*

Flooding is not a survivable event when it comes to sheltering in place. **If your emergency shelter is subject to flooding you cannot stay there**! There are few rare exceptions. One is a boat; the other is to dam the property to keep the waters out. Rising waters from river flooding is one thing. Violent tidal surges associated with a major hurricane are something entirely different. The best option may be to get out (evacuate) if you think your shelter may become subject to tidal surges.

106

The Myth:[7]

- Contemporary weather forecasters using hurricane hunter information and computer modeling can determine where the hurricane will go, and how strong it will be when it makes landfall.

- Since the problem has been foreseen, possibly by as much as a week, government responders will be organized and ready to move into the disaster area immediately as the hurricane moves away.

- Government planners know how long will be required to evacuate a city and travel to areas of relative safety, and can effectively manage a mass exodus from a large metropolitan area.

- People living in high-risk areas will use common sense, prepare and won't have to make last minute emergency purchases of supplies or fuel. There will be enough supplies for everyone in need.

- Hurricane damage is confined to the near-shore area.

The Reality:

- Forecasts only render general direction of hurricanes.

- Hurricanes can and do make unpredictable sharp turns, slow down or speed up.

- Hurricanes also generate severe wind and water damage far inland. Secondary flooding (resulting from rain fall) and tornadoes commonly accompany such storms.

- Government planners operate on a combination of preparation, sound procedures, creative ideas, and hope. They are trained and equipped to work on general problems, not to provide solutions to your personal problems.

Having your own evacuation plan can be a big relief and could help you avoid paying a premium for food, fuel and accommodations and taking a chance on where your family sleeps at night.

---

[7] **From FEMA web site** Evacuation Tips for You and Your Family
Release Date: September 11, 2008
Release Number: 3294-009

Buras, LA, October 25, 2005 - The eye of Hurricane Katrina passed directly over this community. The water tower rests on top of a house in the ruins of Plaquemine Parish. Robert Kaufmann/FEMA

EVACUATION TIPS

Basic Planning Steps

Here are three questions you should answer to get started:

- **Where would you go?** To get out of harm's way, you may need to go north, south, east or west. Pick a destination in each direction. Your primary destination could be with family or friends within the range of one tank full of gas. Stop-and-go driving could drastically reduce how far you can get on a tank of gas, so take that into consideration. **If you decide that you have a safe place to shelter away from harm's way, choose the location well in advance and predetermine how you would get there. Have alternate routes. If you are required to leave via mandatory evacuation, please comply.**

- **Where would you stay?** ⟹ (*Study the Chapter on Where to Shelter*).
    - o Consider the material discussed in the chapter on
    ⟹ **Security** regarding supplies such as food, water and emergency equipment.

- **What would you take with you?** If you need to travel to the place of shelter, have everything ready to go. Pre planning is most critical in these situations.

⇨ *(Study the Checklist and Reference Section).*

- If you don't have reliable transportation of your own, you need to know more in advance about what options are available from your neighbors or local government. Your county emergency manager's (EMA) office is the source for this information. What you can take with you are the same as items as mentioned before, but you are limited by how much you can carry.

Develop a Family Communications Plan

- Scale the plan: Do you need to evacuate your neighborhood, your community or the region.
- Share the plan with family members. Discuss what to do if kids are in school, if a parent is far from home, etc.
- Be sure you have all phone numbers: Work, school, cell phones and land lines, host family, friends, your local emergency management office and/or community evacuation resources.
- Have prearranged radio frequencies outlined and shared with all parties involved.

⇨ *(Study the chapter on Communications).*

Also, see our companion book:
Evacuation: A Family Guide to the 21st Century

NOTES ON TRANSPORTATION, ROUTE PLANNING ETC[8].

Most city governments know (but few will admit it) that it is really not possible for the government even with National Guard assistance to evacuate all residents:

---

[8] Evacuation: A Family Guide for the 21st Century

"**...November 21, 2003**: Study Predicts a Third of New Orleans Residents Would Not Evacuate in Event of Major Hurricane Ivor van Heerden, director of the LSU Center for the Study of the Public Health Impacts of Hurricanes, presents the preliminary findings of a five-year study (see (April 2002)) of the hurricane risk to New Orleans at a special meeting held in the district headquarters of the US Army Corps of Engineers.

The preliminary findings indicate that a third of the city's residents would not evacuate in the event of a major hurricane. Of those who do attempt evacuation, many would get stuck in traffic despite plans to use both sides of the highway. The draft findings also indicate that a major hurricane strike on New Orleans would submerge certain parts of the city under as much as 22 feet of water polluted by a mix of oil, gasoline, and other toxic substances released from myriad storage tanks, cars, trucks, flooded homes, stores, and industrial sites during the storm. Wind would cause damage to most buildings, possibly destroying half of them.

HISTORICAL REVIEW

Here are some reasons to be concerned: Hurricane forecasting is filled with uncertainty.

Hurricane Andrew

The National Hurricane Center is unable to accurately predict a landfall 39 hours, much less 51 hours, before landfall. At 5 am Saturday, 48 hours before landfall, Monroe County (Florida Keys) had not yet ordered an evacuation for Andrew because:

- 48 hours out, Hurricane Andrew was barely a Category 1 storm, having just attained Hurricane classification
- It was incorrectly forecasted to move on shore well to the north near Titusville Florida, and then as a Category 2 storm
- It was not forecasted to move ashore for another 72 hours.

NOTE: Government agencies (state, federal) are somewhat capable of action to correct large infrastructure problems; however counties, cities, and municipalities are the front lines when it comes to restoring basic services. Serious disasters will always overwhelm local jurisdictions, thus slowing their effective response. You may be on your own for weeks, months, or years until the areas is rebuilt or you are forced to resettle in another location.

Question: Is the chaos that accompanies disaster expected by governmental agencies?

Answer: YES it is! Planners know they cannot "control" situations, but the public does not appreciate what that means. Readiness means that the jurisdiction has (or has access to) resources that will answer some needs <u>after</u> the disaster has occurred.

NEW ORLEANS had reviewed the possibility of a hurricane strike.

November 23, 2004-January 31, 2005: Survey Indicates New Orleans Residents May Not Evacuate In Event of Major Hurricane

"....A poll conducted by the University of New Orleans finds that 62 percent of greater New Orleans' 1.3 million residents would feel safe in their homes during a Category 3 storm. Only in the case of a larger Category 4 or 5 hurricanes would a majority of the residents-78 percent-decide to evacuate the city. A total of 401 residents from St. Charles Parish take part in the survey. The figures cause grave concern for the university's researchers who say the results suggest that residents have developed a false sense of security. For decades, residents have successfully ridden out moderate-sized hurricanes. But as University of New Orleans pollster Susan Howell explains, Louisiana's dramatic loss of its coastal wetlands means storms will have a greater impact, thus putting the city's residents at greater risk..." [FEMA compilation from Times-Picayune, 6/23/2005; Times-Picayune, 6/23/2005]

Chapter 13

EARTHQUAKE

Photograph by Dane Golden taken on 01/25/2004 in California (ID: 9390)
Atascadero, CA January 25, 2004 -- This home slid two feet off its foundation due to the 6.5 San Simeon Earthquake. FEMA Photo

I have personally experienced a few minor earthquakes in my life but none of the "big" ones. The thing that generates the most fear is the unpredictability surrounding the event. It is most unsettling to feel the "earth that we live on" shake us like fish in the pan. All that we have come to trust in as "solid" is suddenly demanding reconsideration. This is also one of the hardest scenarios to prepare against as you have literally no warning and no way to prepare for it. It is said that the earthquakes do not kill people it is the buildings they occupy. Be cognizant of this if you live in these areas prone to earthquake. Look at the structure you occupy and do all that you can in advance to make sure it will provide the best protection for your family.

CONSIDER THE FOLLOWING

- **Gas lines:** One of the primary concerns is the risk of fire when gas lines are ruptured and the fumes ignited. If you have a gas water heater, secure it to the surrounding walls with metal straps, and bolting it to the floor to prevent it from tilting over and rupturing the lines.
- **Falling objects**: Look around and imagine what would happen if the things you have hanging on the wall would be shaken loose and fall. Could these objects present a hazard for you or your family? Take particular note to things hanging on, above or near the bed. Often, these events occur at night when we are most vulnerable. Consider anything hung from overhead as a potential hazard, such as heavy light fixtures and chandeliers; reinforce their foundations.
- **Kitchen Cabinets**: Put "child latches" on each of the overhead cabinets to prevent them from falling open allowing its contents to fall to the floor. They may be shaken up a bit but they will remain in the cabinet.
- **Foundations:** In many cases the homes are literally shaken off their foundations making the entire structure unstable. Before it happens, talk to a contractor about securing the frame of the home to its foundations.

PREPARE A PLACE IN ADVANCE FOR COVER

- **Designate a "safe place":**
  - Retrofit a room in the home in the house that would hold up to the event. It can be a bath room or simple archway in the home that could be especially built for this purpose. Define a "safe place" to hide. Depending on your level of concern and propensity to prepare, this could be one central place in the house or several individual places. If it occurs during the night, it may not be enough time to regain sufficient awareness from a deep sleep to go to a central place.

113

- o It may be necessary to locate the kids rooms near the designated "safe place" or to have one located in each of their rooms. These places can be permanent or portable such as a very strong table.
  ⇨ (*Improvise the plans in the Tornado Chapter for Safe Rooms*).

- **Earthquake Table:** Build or buy a piece of furniture that will withstand the weight of falling debris. This may require a compromise between form and function. An attractive cherry wood dining room table would look great with matching chairs in the dining room; but, what would you think of one made of steel? One that could that could support the weight of a collapsed house? Positioned near the center of the main living area, it could save lives. One could easily be made to your specifications and covered with the wood of your choice.

Here is one design currently available.[9]

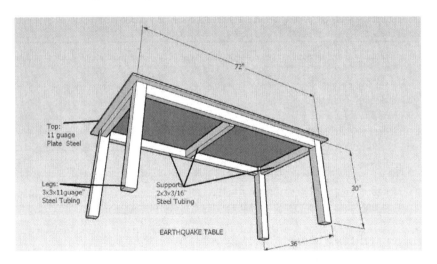

This is a raw piece of steel that would be very heavy but also very strong. A decision needs to be made as to what degree of protection you are comfortable with. You can crawl under a flimsey piece of modern toothpick furniture or have something that will do some good. Modern day furniture is designed to look great but they are mostly made of particle board and Melamine which disentegrates under stress. These plans are simple and could easily be carried to

---

[9] World Disaster Report (www.wdrep.com)

a local welder for construction. It should cost around $500. to build. As mentioned before, the exposed steel could be covered with solid or plywood of your choice, stained and laquered for an elegant look. The only trade off is that it would have very straight lines.

- ○ **Have a 72 hour kit ready and available**. It should be located in a spot where you will run for shelter. ⇨ (*See the Checklist and Reference section on 72 hour kit.*)
- ○ A *hanging shelf* can easily be welded under the surface of the earthquake table to hold this kit or essential supplies such as water and communications devises (whistles, radios,cell phones).

- **Earthquake bed:** To take this idea further, a simple steel frame structure (resembling the earthquake table) could surround the kids bed and double as a "canopy bed". They would just think it was cool and would not know that it could hold support the weight of the family truck. Of course, to allow for the expanded length, specifications in the material would need to be modified.   Also, a "bolt on" configuration would need to be improvised to allow for dissasembly.

Have regular earthquake drills with the family on how to get to the safe place in a hurry. Make a game of it and have some fun. Make it a contest; "hide and seek" in reverse . The first one that gets to the "safe place" (from wherever they are in the house) wins. Chances are the kids will be a formidable adversary in this fun exercise.

Of course, entrapment is always a hazard with this secnario. Consideration for this possibility should be reviewed when thinking about where your "safe place" should be. Think: " If I am trapped here, could we stay for a while?"

⇨ (*Study the Chapter on Medical for items concerning Entrapment).*

Chapter 14

WINTER STORMS

Parsippany, NJ, February 2, 2011 -- Ice forms around tree branches under freezing conditions. Most of Northern New Jersey was under an Ice Storm Warning.

In the winter of 2000, a "100 year blizzard" blanketed the southeastern United States. It was one of the most enjoyable and fun filled times in our family's memory. The entire area was shut down. No one was moving anywhere and nothing was open. Power was out in every direction. I ventured about in my four wheel drive vehicle checking on friends. I found one family huddled up in the corner of their living room floor like puppies against their mothers' belly. They were covered with blankets and shivering from the cold. I invited them to return home with me where we had supplemented all essential services including heat. They refused insisting that they were fine.

What I witnessed was a total breakdown in planning at every level. The family had become completely dependent on the "infrastructure" of public services and was helpless when they were removed. This is the peril of dependency. With a little planning and a change of attitude, these emergency situations can be an enjoyable time filled with lasting family memories. There are two main issues associated with this scenario: Loss of power (heat) and the availability of food supplies.

POWER

The primary hazard associated with this scenario is the loss of power. Ice and snow accumulates on trees and power lines. The additional weight causes them to sag and fall. Tree and branches tumble to the ground and take everything in their path with them. On occasion, these trees and limbs will fall on or through a roof. Then, the storm is in your home and not just on it. Hopefully, you will have made the preparations so that when this eventuality occurs, all you have to do is to hook up a generator and throw a switch.

In most cases, this situation will not last very long. The utilities have a lot of experience dealing with these storms. Cooperative agreements are in place between neighboring communities, states and entire regions to send helpful resources where needed. The outages are usually hours to days; rarely weeks. The more rural environments will usually face the longest outages as resources are utilized to restore the more populated areas first. Therefore, if you know that you are in the situation where you may be last on the list, make the necessary preparations to take care of yourself.

⬜⟹ (*See the chapter on Electrical*)

FOOD AND WATER

The other consequence of the loss of power is that the food in the refrigerator and freezer is in danger. The good part about this scenario is that it is cold outside. If the power is out long enough, you can simply move the food to the back porch, in the shade where the temperatures are lowest. Hopefully, this will not be necessary. In most cases food in the frig will be good for a few days if you limit the times you open the door. The frig becomes an oversized cooler. The items in it are cool and will stay that way until it is eventually overcome by room temperature.

The food in the freezer should stay cold for a long time. This is especially true if it is a chest type and is full. The hardened frozen food in the freezer becomes its own ice chest. Depending on the temperature of the outside air and quality of the freezer the contents should stay good for a week or so. Remember not to open the freezer door more than necessary. Plan exactly what you want and where it may be before you open the door.

Again, it is important that a supply of food be on hand prior to the storms arrival. It is typical that as soon as the announcement of the storm is made by the weather service, the super markets are flooded with those wishing to stock up on necessary supplies: chips, beer, soft drinks, salsa..........OK and maybe some milk and bread.

It is difficult to comfortably live through an emergency if we never consider it a possibility. Have a different mindset. Buy more food than you need and store it little by little. Rotate it often so that when you need it, it is there.

⇨ *(See the chapter on Food and Water)*

INSURANCE

If your home is damaged during the storm, you will most always be authorized to make immediate repairs to prevent further damage to the property. Insurance companies do not want to pay for a loss that was once small that became larger because it was not dealt with early on. Have tarps and roofing nails on hand to do the job. You will most always be authorized by the insurance carrier to make temporary repairs to prevent the damage from becoming larger.

⇨ *(See the chapter on Insurance)*

ON THE ROAD

The winter storms of 2011 forced many of us to consider our level of preparation for this scenario. The weight of snow forced many roofs to collapse including the Metrodome in Minneapolis, MN. Countless residential roofs also collapsed in an "unusual" winter. It appears however, that the frequency of the "unusual" events is increasing to the point where the unusual is becoming usual.

Be prepared for the unexpected: the unusual. It was unusual for Lakeshore Drive, near Chicago, to become a snow bank filled with stranded motorist but it happened in the winter of 2011. Many were trapped in their cars as snow fell around them. Eventually, they could not move and were running out of gas. On a normal commute home from work, they could have lost their lives.

How hard would it have been to have some emergency supplies in the car "just in case"? A "go bag" kept in the trunk of the car, could have been the difference between life and death. It is easy to assemble and maintain. Make it happen! Put it in the trunk and leave it there. Care needs to be taken however, to prevent the water from freezing and breaking its container and the small food rations to stay current. Other than that it is trouble free. Leave blankets and an extra supply of warm clothes in a separate bag. You may be very glad you did!

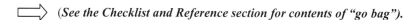 (*See the Checklist and Reference section for contents of "go bag"*).

In addition to the things listed there, you will need a emergency road supplies:

- Shovel (military style collapsible if space is an issue)
- Chain (tow strap)
- Emergency flairs
- Glass scraper, and small broom
- Booster cables
- Emergency Flairs
- Fluorescent distress flag
- Snow boots with thick wool socks
- Gloves, sock hat, wool scarf
- Ax or Hatchet

Also, remember to give the car proper attention. It is the craft that will transport you from harm to home. Make it reliable!

Chapter 15

NUCLEAR

Edinburgh, IN, March 13, 2011 -- Contingents from the FEMA Region IV and National Incident Management Assistance Team-West and other FEMA personnel mobilized to Indiana to support a large-scale, multi-agency chemical, biological, radiological, nuclear, explosive (CBRNE) exercise A standard component of every American soldiers training includes: NBC (Nuclear, Biological, and Chemical).

During our military NBC (Nuclear, Biological, Chemical) training, we would often joke among ourselves that the only purpose in the training was to prolong our life just enough to provide one last gesture of resistance to the enemy. The training exposes some of the most deadly and heinous forms of warfare known to man.

Our intent in this section is to give you the information that would be most likely needed when in proximity to nuclear power plants and spills during transportation. There are multiple redundant safety systems in place in every American Nuclear power station and we should all feel very safe to be near them. Having training on how hazardous material is transported gives me confidence that we should all be more concerned traveling next to a fuel truck than next to one of the federal waste transports.

NUCLEAR POWER PLANT INCIDENT PLANNING

What exactly should you do if asked to take shelter?

- If you live within 100 miles of a nuclear power plant, you should have a definite family plan that addresses this problem. The plan must incorporate your specific needs, as well as address the generic measures that are recommended by the government.

- Potassium Iodide (or potassium Iodate) is effective to minimize the risk of thyroid contamination by radioisotopes. Consider having a supply of this on hand in your first aid container. See detail on this subject below in this section.

- A nuclear incident at a power plant does not have the same effects as a nuclear bomb. Depending on your proximity to the plant, you may very well be able to remain in your home.

- Even after an emergency has been announced, you may still have a number of hours to take care of last minute preparations before contamination actually occurs.

- Prevailing wind, presence or absence of rain, as well as other atmospheric factors will determine just how much contamination your specific area will experience. There is no way to predict this in detail until the event actually occurs.

- Government radiation monitoring will likely give information for a geographical area, not your specific location.

- Remain indoors. Close all external doors and windows. Turn off all air-conditioning or ventilating devices that might draw in outside air. Air conditioning can be used if set to recirculate inside air. Sealing windows and doors with duct tape and thin plastic may dramatically reduce risk of contamination. Using gas fired heating systems may not be possible since they consume oxygen (creating danger of asphyxiation) unless sufficient outside air is available. Therefore you may have to do without heat if contamination is severe. Stand alone floor or desk-type fans are OK to use.

- Government publications recommend that you listen to your local radio for further instructions. Do not leave your shelter or evacuate unless told to do so. If you have amateur radio (2 meter HAM or short wave) you may be able to get more timely and accurate information from those operators.

- If you must go outside, limit your total exposure time to half an hour or less. Wear an N-100 rated protective mask. If you have no mask, cover your mouth and nose with layers of cloth while you are outside.

- The following tables show how various materials can stop different levels of radiation. (Courtesy U.S. Nuclear Regulatory Commission).

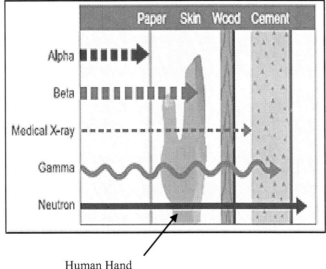

Human Hand

This table shows that you can protect yourself by using common sense and materials at hand in your own home.

- Your actual risk depends on the amount of exposure and the type to radiation to which you are exposed.

Remember the following critical factors:

- **Distance** - The more distance between you and the source of the radiation, the better. This could be evacuation or remaining indoors to minimize exposure.
- **Shielding** - The heavier, dense material between you and the source of the radiation, the better.
- **Time** – Depending on the materials involved, radioactive particles loses strength more quickly than you might think.
- **Alpha particles** are charged particles, which are also emitted from naturally occurring materials (such as uranium, thorium, and radium) and man-made elements (such as plutonium and americium). Alpha particles have a very limited ability to penetrate other materials. These particles of ionizing radiation can be blocked by a sheet of paper, skin, or even a few inches of air. Alpha particles do not usually make anything radioactive. Nonetheless, <u>materials that emit alpha particles are potentially dangerous if they are inhaled or swallowed</u>, but external exposure generally does not pose a danger.
- **Beta particles** are similar to electrons and are emitted from naturally occurring materials (such as strontium-90). Some beta emitters are used in medical applications. These beta particles are lighter than alpha particles, and they generally have a greater ability to penetrate other materials. These particles can travel a few feet in the air, and can penetrate skin. A thin sheet of metal or plastic or a block of wood can stop beta particles. Like alpha particles, they do not usually make things radioactive. **Beta particles are dangerous if inhaled or swallowed.**
- **Gamma and X-rays** consist of high-energy waves that can travel great distances at the speed of light and generally have a great ability to penetrate other materials. For that reason, gamma rays (such as from cobalt-60) are often used in medical applications to treat cancer and sterilize medical instruments. Similarly, x-rays are typically used to provide static images of body parts (such as teeth and bones) and are also used in industry to find defects in welds. Despite their ability to penetrate other materials, in general, neither gamma rays nor x-rays have the ability to make anything radioactive. Several feet of concrete or a few inches of dense material (such as lead) are able to block these types of radiation. **Neutrons** are high-speed nuclear particles that have an exceptional ability to penetrate other materials. Of the five types of ionizing radiation discussed here, neutrons are the only one that can make objects radioactive. This process, called

neutron activation produces many of the radioactive sources that are used in medical, academic and industrial applications (including oil exploration).

Because of their exceptional ability to penetrate other materials, neutrons can travel great distances in air and require very thick hydrogen-containing materials (such as concrete or water) to block them. Fortunately, neutron radiation primarily occurs inside a nuclear reactor, where many feet of water provide effective shielding.

Use of Potassium Iodide (U.S. Nuclear Regulatory Commission, www.nrc.gov)

In January 2001, the Commission published a rule change to the NRC (Nuclear Regulatory Commission) emergency planning regulations to include the consideration of the use of potassium iodide. If taken properly, potassium iodide (KI) will help reduce the dose of radiation to the thyroid gland from radioactive iodine and reduce the risk of thyroid cancer. The Food and Drug Administration (FDA) has issued guidance on the dosage and effectiveness of potassium iodide.

The NRC has supplied KI tablets to States requesting it for the population within the 10-mile emergency planning zone. If necessary, KI is to be used to supplement evacuation or sheltering in place, not to take the place of these actions. If radioactive iodine is taken into the body after consumption of potassium iodide, it will be rapidly excreted from the body. For more information, see Consideration of use of potassium iodide in nuclear emergencies.

The population closest to the nuclear power plant that is within the 10-mile emergency planning zone is at greatest risk of exposure to radiation and radioactive materials. When the population is evacuated out of the area and potentially contaminated foodstuffs are removed from the market, the risk from further radioactive iodine exposure to the thyroid gland is essentially eliminated. Beyond 10 miles, the major risk of radioiodine exposure is from ingestion of contaminated foodstuffs, particularly milk products. Both the Environmental Protection Agency (EPA) and the FDA have published guidance to protect consumers from contaminated foods. These protective actions are preplanned in the 50-mile ingestion pathway EPZ.

Remember, in the unlikely event of a nuclear power plant accident, it is important to follow the direction of your State or local government in order to make sure protective actions, such as taking potassium iodide pills, are implemented safely and effectively for the affected population.

This may help you to understand how a nuclear emergency may be classified as it evolves.

- **Emergency Classification (per U.S. Nuclear Regulatory Commission, www.nrc.gov)**

An Emergency Classification is a set of plant conditions which indicate a level of risk to the public. Both nuclear power plants and research and test reactors use the four emergency classifications listed below in order of increasing severity. The vast majority of events reported to the NRC are routine in nature and do not require activation of our incident response program. For information on how we respond to an event that could threaten public health and safety, see **How We Respond To an Emergency.**

Recognizing that security-related events may involve different response actions from the licensees, the NRC issued Bulletin 2005-02, Emergency Preparedness and Response Actions for Security-Based Events. This bulletin identifies minor changes to the emergency classification levels to reflect emphasis of post-9/11 conditions.

- **Notification of Unusual Event -** Under this category, events are in process or have occurred which indicate *potential degradation in the level of safety of the plant*. No release of radioactive material requiring offsite response or monitoring is expected unless further degradation occurs.
- **Alert -** If an alert is declared, events are in process or have occurred which involve an actual or potential substantial degradation in the level of safety of the plant. Any releases of radioactive material from the plant are expected to be limited to a small fraction of the Environmental Protection Agency (EPA) protective action guides (PAGs) .
- **Site Area Emergency -** A site area emergency involves events in process or which have occurred that result in actual or likely major failures of plant functions needed for protection of the public. Any releases of radioactive material are not expected to exceed the EPA PAGs except near the site boundary.
- **General Emergency -** A general emergency involves actual or imminent substantial core damage or melting of reactor fuel with the potential for loss of containment integrity. Radioactive releases during a general emergency can reasonably be expected to exceed the EPA PAGs for more than the immediate site area.

The following are emergency classifications for nuclear materials and fuel cycle facility licensees:

125

- **Alert** - Events may occur, are in progress or have occurred that could lead to a release of radioactive material(s) but the release is not expected to require a response by an offsite response organization to protect people offsite.

- **Site Area Emergency** - Events may occur, are in progress, or have occurred that could lead to a significant release of radioactive material[s], and the release could require a response by offsite response organizations to protect people offsite.

GENERAL NOTES ON NUCLEAR POWER PLANTS:

The majority of nuclear power plants in the United States, if not across the world, are Pressured Water Reactors (PWR). Simply put, the heat produced through the fission process boils the water that creates the steam that runs the turbines and produces electricity. There are three layers of protection against a leak or radioactive materials. The fuel rods themselves are encased in a Zirconium Alloy which is then placed in a steel casing reactor pressure vessel. This is all encased in a one foot thick concrete and steel dome reinforced with multiple layers of rebar and wire cables.

There is not enough of the right kind of nuclear material in these plants to cause a nuclear explosion. If there ever was an explosive event, it would be a result of a buildup in hydrogen or steam. The fuel rods are kept cool by pumps and running water. If the pumps lose offsite (commercial) power, backup diesel generators automatically kick in. Behind the emergency generators there are a series of battery banks that would provide power for a limited number of hours. If all systems fail, the station goes into what is called a "station blackout". That is where the real problems exist and is exactly what happened at the Fukushima power plant in Futaba, Japan.

In April 2011 the Browns Ferry nuclear power station near Huntsville, Alabama suffered a direct hit form a tornado knocking it off line. The emergency generators kicked in and the plant initiated a "cold shutdown" within 72 hours. There was never an emergency and the systems operated as they were designed to do.

In the aftermath of the Fukushima event, the NRC is recommending that a set of portable backup generators be positioned in the United States where they can be delivered to any plant at risk within 24 hours. As a result of the extreme precautions and safeguards in place to protect the public, these nuclear power plants represent a miniscule risk.

SOME NOTES ON THE FUKISHIMA INCIDENT

The Mainichi Daily News
"...David Boilley, president of the Acro radioactivity measuring body, said at a press conference in Tokyo that the results of the survey on 10 boys and girls in Fukushima City aged between 6 and 16 suggest there is a high possibility that children in and near the city have been exposed to radiation internally..." **July 26, 2011**

Nishio Masamichi, Tokyo Keizai, July 1, 2011
Necessary Countermeasures:
1. Among people living in the same area, rates of exposure can vary greatly based on lifestyle and movement patterns. As a result, it is important that every resident in at risk areas be given a device to monitor personal radiation exposure. Apart from protecting individuals and allowing them to make informed decisions about their safety, the data gathered can be used in future medical research and in court cases that will no doubt originate from the Fukushima Daiichi accident.
2. There is little conclusive scientific data on the risks of low level radiation exposure. The government; however, must not let this turn into a case of "we don't know so we can assume it is safe". On the contrary, Nishio argues that it is necessary to proceed under the assumption "we don't know so we must assume that it is dangerous".
3. Residents must be given real time radiation data as well as the best possible advice about how to decrease their exposure.
4. While there are limits to what this can achieve, dirt from schoolyards should be regularly removed and replaced.
5. Strontium 90, which has a half-life of 28.7 years and can have a serious impact on child bone development, must be carefully measured.
6. In planning of future solutions, radiation effects on the body should take priority over the potential stresses associated with relocation.
7. The government should buy houses and land in irradiated areas at pre-crisis market value and provide additional aid for resettlement. Cleanup measures should be undertaken and when the areas become safe, the government should sell property back at reduced rates. A respect for both present necessity and the deep attachment that many have to land that has been in their families for many generations is necessary if the government wants to convince nuclear refugees that they are being treated fairly.

8. The government should make every effort to provide accurate information, but should not forcibly remove elderly residents who wish to remain in their homes.

Results of ACRO's monitoring in Japan (25th July 2011 update)

- The contamination is very large and comparable to the environment of Chernobyl.
- The Maeda field of Iitate-mura is the most contaminated place.
- Iodine contamination is the largest and it is better to evacuate the population.
- On the long time range, cesium 137 is the most worrying element because it has a half-life of 30 years.
- Regarding the results expressed in Bq/kg of soil, most of them are higher than the limit fixed by the Japanese authorities at 5 000 Bq/kg for agriculture. Rice cannot be cultivated.

The data expressed in Bq/m² can be compared to the definition of the zones in Byelorussia after the Chernobyl disaster (law of 1991) :
185 000 - 555 000 Bq/m²: migration allowed
555 000 - 1 480 000 Bq/m²: right to re-housing

Most of the results are higher than one of these limits.
Fragmentary quote from April 11, 2011 report

Summary:

- Do not breathe, eat contaminated dust, or allow it to remain on the skin. Use masks and protective over-clothing if you must move around outside after a release has occurred.

- If you must travel by automobile through a contaminated area, before beginning the journey, seal the external automobile's air intakes (for the passenger compartment) with tape. It may be very difficult if not impossible to seal the passenger compartment from outside air. This should be considered before you think about venturing about. Once sealing has been completed, using the air conditioner or heater (with the control set on recirculation of inside air) will not create additional exposure risk.

- Emergency instructions via commercial radio will advise the official emergency status. If you go outside and are exposed to a radioactive release for more than 1/2 hour, change (bag and discard your old) clothing and shower thoroughly as a prudent precaution. Be sure to wash hair and beneath fingernails carefully and thoroughly.

- Sealing your house
  - This is useful only when contamination is severe.
  - Use duct tape and thin plastic (paint drop cloth) for windows and doors. This takes more tape than you might imagine.

- Radiation effects on animals
  - Pets and farm animals are just as susceptible to radiation as humans. Placing animals in barns may help some to diminish contamination.

- Contamination of food
  - Direct contamination of vegetables and other exposed food stuffs is the main hazard. Canned foods are safe as long as the cans are washed before being handled and opened.

- Contamination of water
  - Contaminated dust may fall into open water (municipal reservoirs) making that water unsafe.
  - Conventional water filtration will not remove radioactive contamination. Water storage is necessary to circumvent this problem.

Chapter 16

VOLCANO

Mt. St. Helens, WA, May 18, 1980 -- Disasters are devastating to the natural and man-made environment. FEMA provides federal aid and assistance to those who have been affected by all types of disaster. NOAA News Photo (source: asgs.gov)

Having business in the American northwest, I was able to see Mt St. Helens before and after the eruption. The power of the event, despite the turmoil and destruction, was nothing short of awe-inspiring. A major eruption anywhere in the world could have worldwide implications. This is a scenario that all of us need to be aware of and prepared for. The balance of the material in this chapter is information provided by governmental agencies.[10]

When ash begins to fall during daylight hours, the sky will turn increasingly hazy and "dusty" and sometimes a pale yellow color. The falling ash may become so dense that daylight turns to murky gray or even an "intense blackness" such that "it is impossible to see your hand when held up close to the eye." Loud thunder and lightning and the strong smell of sulfur often occurs during an ash fall. Furthermore, rain may accompany the ash and turn the tiny particles into a slurry of slippery mud. Most people also describe an intense quietness, except for thunder that may accompany the ash fall, giving "deadness" to the normal sounds of life.

Volcanic ash is rock that has been pulverized into dust or sand by volcanic activity. In very large eruptions, ash is accompanied by rocks having the weight and density of hailstones. Volcanic ash is hot near the volcano, but it is cool when it falls at greater distances

GENERAL PRINCIPLES[11]

- Volcanic eruptions are relatively rare, but often deadly when they occur. Think ahead and follow your instincts. It is much better to leave early and

---

[10] [10] **Oregon Department of Geology and Mineral Industries (web site)**
800 NE Oregon St.
Portland, OR 97232
(971) 673-1555

Washington State Military Department, Emergency Management Division, and the USGS Cascades Volcano Observatory, 1999

[11] **Oregon Department of Geology and Mineral Industries (web site)**
800 NE Oregon St.
Portland, OR 97232
(971) 673-1555

Washington State Military Department, Emergency Management Division, and the USGS Cascades Volcano Observatory, 1999

return after a minor eruption subsides than to become part of a modern Pompeii or Herculaneum if the eruption turns out to be "the big one".

- Remember that statistical estimates of times between eruptions represent historical data and are not predictions. When the magma begins to move, history becomes irrelevant.
- Know in advance what to expect and how to deal with it; that will make it manageable.
- In ashy areas, use dust masks and eye protection. If you don't have a dust mask, use a wet handkerchief.
- Stay indoors to minimize exposure -- especially if you have respiratory ailments.
- Minimize travel -- driving in ash is hazardous to you and your car.
- Use your radio for information on the ash fall.
- Keep ash out as much as possible.
- The most effective method to prevent ash-induced damage to machinery is to shut down, close off or seal equipment until ash is removed from the immediate environment, but this may not be practical in all cases, especially for critical facilities.
- Coordinate clean-up activities with neighbors and community-wide operations (learn the clean-up guidelines and instructions of your local community and leaders).
- Stay informed of volcanic activity in your area, especially during periods of unrest, and knows what to expect, including the type of eruptions that can occur and how much warning is possible for ash fall in your area once an explosive eruption occurs. Learn about evacuation procedures, if any, in your area.
- Prepare for an emergency by having critical provisions and supplies needed to support your family, business, or community for at least several days; for example, food, water, medicine, and shelter, dust masks and other personal protection equipment, spare filters and parts for machinery and vehicles.
- Develop and test a contingency plan that can be used in a variety of emergencies, but not necessarily focused on volcanoes.

WHAT TO DO:

Before ash fall:

Essential items to stock

A sustained ash fall may keep people housebound for hours or even days. Keep these items in your home in case of an ash fall:

- Dust masks and eye protection. (See Recommended Masks, from the International Volcanic Health Hazard Network).
- Enough drinking water for at least 72 hours (one gallon per person per day).
- Enough non-perishable food for at least 72 hours for family and pets.
- Plastic wrap (to keep ash out of electronics).
- Battery-operated radio and extra batteries.
- Lanterns or flashlights and extra batteries.
- If cold, extra wood for a fireplace or stove.
- If cold, extra blankets and warm clothing.
- Extra stocks of medication for both family and pets.
- First aid kit.
- Cleaning supplies (broom, vacuum cleaner & bags/filters, shovels etc.).
- Small amount of money (ATM machines may not be working).
- Consider that you could be stuck in your vehicle, so store emergency supplies in your vehicle too.

Your home

- Close doors and windows.
- Place damp towels at door thresholds and other draft sources. Tape drafty windows.
- Protect sensitive electronics and do not uncover until the environment is totally ash-free.
- Disconnect drainpipes/downspouts from gutters to stop drains clogging, but allowing ash and water to empty from gutters onto the ground.
- If you use a rainwater collection system for your water supply, disconnect the tank prior to ash falling.
- If you have chronic bronchitis, emphysema or asthma, stay inside and avoid unnecessary exposure to the ash.

Your Children

- Explain what a volcano is and what they should expect and do if ash falls.
- Know your school's emergency plan.
- Have quiet games and activities available.

Your pets

- Ensure livestock have clean food and water.
- Store extra food and drinking water.
- Keep extra medicine on hand.
- Keep your animals under cover, if possible.

Your car

Any vehicle can be considered a movable, second home. Always carry a few items in your vehicle in case of delays, emergencies, or mechanical failures.

- Dust masks and eye protection.
- Blankets and extra clothing.
- Emergency food and drinking water.
- General emergency supplies: first aid kit, flashlight, fire extinguisher, took lit, flares, matches, survival manual, etc.
- Waterproof tarp, heavy tow rope.
- Extra air and oil filters, extra oil, windshield wiper blades and windshield washer fluid.
- Cell phone with extra battery.

During and after ash fall

- Do not wear contact lenses as these can result in corneal abrasion.
- If there is ash in your water, let it settle and then use the clear water. If there is a lot of ash in the water supply, do not use your dishwasher or washing machine. Water contaminated by ash will usually make drinking water unpalatable before it presents a health risk.
- You may eat vegetables from the garden, but wash them first.
- Minimize driving and other activities that stir ash.
- Remove as much ash as you can from frequently used areas. Clean from the top down. Wear a dust mask.
- Prior to sweeping, dampen ash to ease removal. Be careful to not wash ash into drainpipes, sewers, storm drains, etc.

- Use water sparingly. Widespread use of water for clean-up may deplete public water supply.
- Seek advice from public officials regarding disposal of volcanic ash in your community.
- Wet ash can be slippery. Use caution when climbing on ladders and roofs.

Notes:

In general, surfaces should be vacuumed to remove as much ash as possible from carpets, furniture, office equipment, appliances, and other items. Portable vacuum systems equipped with high-efficiency particulate filtering systems are recommended whenever possible. The severity of ash intrusion depends on the integrity of windows and entrances, the air intake features, and the care exercised to control the transport of ash into a building or home via shoes and clothing. Care should also be taken to avoid further contamination during the emptying, cleaning, and maintenance of vacuum equipment.

Fresh volcanic ash is gritty, abrasive, sometimes corrosive, and always unpleasant. Although ash is not highly toxic, it can trouble infants, the elderly and those with respiratory ailments. Small ash particles can abrade the front of the eye under windy and ashy conditions.

Ash abrades and jams machinery. It contaminates and clogs ventilation, water supplies and drains. Ash also causes electrical short circuits -- in transmission lines (especially when wet), in computers, and in microelectronic devices. Power often goes out during and after ash fall.

Long-term exposure to wet ash can corrode metal. Exposure to ash can cause respiratory distress or complete respiratory collapse and death.

Ash accumulates like heavy snowfall, but doesn't melt. The weight of ash can cause roofs to collapse. A one-inch layer of ash weighs 5-10 pounds per square foot when dry, but 10-15 pounds per square foot when wet. Wet ash is slippery. Ash re-suspended by wind, and human activity, and can disrupt lives for months after an eruption.

Why should we clean up the ash?

Volcanic ash is a great nuisance and gets everywhere in the house and office, including inside televisions, computers, cameras and other valuable equipment, where it can cause irreparable damage. Ash is different from ordinary house dust. Its sharp, crystalline structure causes it to scratch and abrade surfaces when

135

it is removed by wiping or brushing. In wet weather the ash deposits are dampened down and the air can be clear, but in drier weather ash can easily be stirred up and remobilized by wind and traffic. As a result suspended dust levels become much higher and can be at levels potentially harmful to health. Rainfall and wind are effective in removing the ash and grass and other plants will eventually bind it to the soil, but with large ash falls this process is too slow and the ash must be cleaned up and taken away from populated areas. In addition, wind may also bring ash into areas which were previously clean so ash may be present in the environment for months or even years following an eruption.

What precautions should be taken before cleaning up ash?

Those undertaking clean-up operations should always wear effective dust masks (see recommended masks from the International Volcanic Health Hazard Network). In fine-ash environments, wear goggles or corrective eyeglasses instead of contact lenses to protect eyes from irritation. Lightly water down the ash deposits before they are removed by shoveling, being careful not to excessively wet the deposits on roofs, causing excess loading and danger of collapse.

Dry brushing can produce very high exposure levels and should be avoided. Use extra precaution on ladders and roofs. The ash makes surfaces much more slippery, consequently many people have died from falls while cleaning ash from their roofs. Be aware of the extra load caused by standing on an already overloaded roof - tread carefully. It is preferable to clean roofs before more than a few centimeters of ash has accumulated. Where possible use a harness.

OUTSIDE

Do

- Put on a recommended mask before starting to clean. If you don't have one, use a wet cloth. Wearing protective eye wear (such as goggles) during clean-up is also advised in dry conditions.
- Moisten the ash with a sprinkler, before attempting to clean. This will help to stop the wind remobilizing it.
- Use shovels for removing the bulk of thick deposits of ash (over 1 cm or so), stiff brooms will be required to remove lesser amounts.
- Place the ash into heavy duty plastic bags, or onto trucks if available.
- Since most roofs cannot support more than four inches (10 cm) of wet ash, keep roofs free of thick accumulation.
- Volcanic ash is slippery. Use caution when climbing on ladders and roofs.

- Guttering systems clog very easily so, if fitted underneath your roof, sweep away from the gutters.
- Cut grass and hedges only after rain or light sprinkling and bag clippings.
- Seek advice from public officials regarding disposal of volcanic ash in your community. In most cases, ash should be separated from normal rubbish for collection for disposal at a designated location-mixing ash with normal rubbish can result in damage to collection vehicles and take up space in landfills.
- Dampen ash in yards and streets to reduce suspension of ash, however try to use water sparingly - do not soak the ash. Widespread use of water for clean-up may deplete public water supplies. Follow requests from public officials regarding water use during cleanup operations.
- Remove outdoor clothing before entering a building.

Don't

- Do not soak the ash as it will cake into a hard mass, making cleanup more difficult. On roofs the added weight of the water will increase the risk of roof collapse.
- Do not dump the ash in gardens or on the roadside.
- Do not wash the ash into the guttering, sewers or storm drains. (It can damage waste water treatment systems and clog pipes).
- Do not drive unless absolutely necessary, driving stirs up the ash. Furthermore, ash is harmful to vehicles.

INSIDE

Do
- Clean your house when public-works crews are cleaning the areas outside your house as a coordinated approach. Put on your mask before starting to clean. If you don't have one, use a wet cloth. Ensure good ventilation by opening all doors and windows before you start to clean.
- Only use one entrance to the building while cleaning to ensure occupants do not bring in ash into clean areas.
- Use a dustless method of cleaning such as washing with water and an effective detergent/wetting agent. Damp rag techniques or vacuuming should be used whenever possible. After vacuuming, carpets and upholstery may be cleaned with a detergent shampoo. Avoid excess rubbing action because the sharp ash particles may cut textile fibers.
- Glass, porcelain enamel and acrylic surfaces may be scratched if wiped too vigorously. Use a detergent soaked cloth or sponge and dab rather than wipe.

137

- High-shine wood finishes will be dulled by the fine grit. Vacuum surfaces and then blot with a wet cloth. A tack cloth used by furniture refinishers should also work well.
- Ash-coated fabrics should either be rinsed under running water and washed carefully, or they can be taken outside and beaten to remove the ash.
- Soiled clothing will require extra detergent. Wash small loads of clothing, using plenty of water so the clothes will have room to move freely in the water. Brush or shake clothes before washing.
- Moisten thick ash deposits on hard floors and place in bags (avoid sweeping dry ash).
- Use a damp mop or wet cloth to clean hard floors.
- Clean your computer, TV and radio equipment using a vacuum cleaner or compressed air. Switch off the main power supply to the machine before carrying out this operation.
- For several months after an ash fall, filters may need replacing often. Air conditioner and furnace filters need careful attention. Clean refrigerator air intakes. Clean any surface that may blow air and recirculate the ash. Stove fans and vents should be cleaned thoroughly.
- Keep children indoors and discourage play in dusty settings.
- Keep pets indoors. If pets go out, brush them before letting them indoors.

Don't

- Do not use floor sweepers with side brushes to clear aisles and floors because they may re-entrain dust particles into the air.
- Do not clean by blowing with compressed air or dry sweeping as ash will be remobilized into the air.
- Do not use fans or electric clothes dryers which might remobilize ash.

VEHICLES

- If possible, avoid driving as ash is harmful to vehicles, the roads may be slippery and driving suspends ash into the air which causes low visibility and may be harmful or irritating to others.
- If driving is crucial, drive slowly, use headlights and ample windscreen fluid. Using wipers on dry ash may scratch the windscreen. In heavier ash fall driving should only be undertaken in an emergency. Use water bottles and a cloth to clean the windscreen as required, this may be every few tens of meters.
- Change oil and oil filters frequently (every 50-100 miles in heavy dust; every 500-1000 miles in light dust).

- Do not drive without an air filter. If you cannot change it, clean it by blowing air from the inside out.
- Cleaning your car - clean ash from inside your engine, trunk/boot and spare tire storage area as well as the seating area. Brushing ash off the car can cause scratching.
- Have a service garage clean wheel brake assemblies every 50-100 miles for very severe road conditions, or every 200-500 miles for heavy dust conditions. The brake assemblies should be cleaned with compressed air.
- Have service garage clean alternators with compressed air after heavy accumulation, every 500 to 1000 miles, or after severe dust exposure.
- Clean the vehicle, including the engine, radiator, and other essential parts daily, if necessary, using water to flush the ash.
- Wash the engine compartment with a garden hose or steam cleaner. Be sure Policy and management measures that reduce the likelihood of damage or failure of equipment from volcanic ash.

- Engineering design measures that reduce vulnerability to ash.
- Preparedness and response planning to deal with ash fall and clean-up activities.

References

Baxter, P.J., 1986, Preventive Health Measures in Volcanic Eruptions. American Journal of Public Health 76 (1986) Supplement: 84-90.

Baxter, P.J. and Maynard, R.L., 1998, Health criteria for reoccupation of ashfall areas in Montserrat. October 1998.

Blong, R.J., 1984, Volcanic hazards: a sourcebook on the effects of eruptions: Academic Press, Australia, 424 p.

Cascades Volcano Observatory and Washington State Emergency Management Division, 1999, volcanic ash fall: how to be prepared for an ash fall: U.S. Geological Survey and Washington Military Department Emergency Management Division, 1 p.

The Emergency Department, St John's, 1998, Resident's guide to the state of the Soufrière Hills volcano following the scientific assessment of July 1998 and the dangers of volcanic ash with tips for cleaning up ash. Montserrat, West Indies. August 1998.

Federal Emergency Management Agency (FEMA), 1984, The mitigation of ash fall damage to public facilities: lessons learned from the 1980 eruption of Mount St. Helens, Washington. Region X, Wm. H. Mayer, Regional Director. 1984.

FEMA/USGS, 1999, volcanic ash fall: How to be prepared for an ash fall. November 1999.

Johnston, D., and Becker, J., 2001, Volcanic ash review - Part 1: impacts on lifelines services and collection/disposal issues: Auckland Regional Council Technical Publication No. 144, 50 p. (http://www.aelg.org.nz/publications.htm#aelg13)

Lauer, S.E., 1995, Pumice and ash, an account of the 1994 Rabaul volcanic eruptions: CPD Resources, Australia, 80 p.

Mt. St. Helens Technical Information Network, 1980, Ash particles and home clean-up problems; advice from the University of Idaho. Bulletin 7. Federal Coordinating Network, May 1980.

Zais, R., 1999, City of Yakima: Presentation on the eruption of Mount St. Helens to Regional Council Civil Defense in New Plymouth, New Zealand.

|| Accessibility || FOIA || Privacy || Policies and Notices ||

URL: http://volcanoes.usgs.gov/ash/todo.html
Page Contact Information: GS-G-HI_Ash@usgs.gov
Page Last Modified: Tuesday, 3 February 2009

Oregon Department of Geology and Mineral Industries (web site)
800 NE Oregon St.
Portland, OR 97232
(971) 673-1555

Washington State Military Department, Emergency Management Division, and the USGS Cascades Volcano Observatory, 1999

Chapter 17

CIVIL UNREST

Army National Guard

In this scenario security is the greatest concern. It is the most unpredictable, volatile and dangerous scenario to consider. The bulk of the recommendations associated with this scenario would be covered in that material.

⇨   *(Study the chapter on Security)*

The bottom line is that if you are in an area where civil unrest may erupt, you should consider leaving: Evacuate! It may be necessary for you to "stay put for a while. Do you have enough food, water and supplies to hold out?

⇨   *(Study the chapter on Food and Water)*

If you have to stay for an extended period of time it may be necessary for you to go out and acquire supplies.

⇨   *(Study the chapter on Getting Around)*

If you do decide to stay consider the following points.

- Cities can be extremely dangerous during periods of civil disorder. There will never be enough police to control a large armed mob. Leaving for a predetermined safe area is the only option if rioting occurs.
- If rioting has actually begun, it is best to stay put. You do not want to become entangled in a rowdy crowd.
- Riots often "burn themselves out" in a matter of hours or days. If local infrastructure damage is not excessive, you may be able to return within a short period of time.
- Maintaining contact with responsible neighbors will help you maintain situational awareness, provide a possible warning of trouble (don't necessarily wait for civil authorities to declare a problem) and provide mutual assistance as trouble unfolds. Choose your shelters carefully so that you will not have to relocate during what may be a very inopportune time.

During these times the rioters feel that they are free to do whatever they want to do because there are no consequences. This is the attitude that makes the situation most dangerous. It is simply not a place that you need to be close to.

Chapter 18

PANDEMIC

Baton Rouge, La., October 9, 2005 - A "victim" of a chemical spill training session is rescued by members of an area Emergency Medical Technician team during a training exercise for first responders to hazardous materials and toxic contamination situations. Chemical and other toxic material conditions caused by Hurricanes Katrina and Rita are cleaned up by personnel who have undergone similar training. Win Henderson / FEMA

This scenario has the potential to present the most serious and long lasting emergency situation. There have been dramatizations presented on various media programs depicting what life would be like during and after such an event in the worse case scenario. As the following chart shows, it would probably come in waves.

During and between these occurrences, would be the time to reevaluate your situation regarding where you are and where you want to be when the next wave strikes. The results are unpredictable and troublesome but the best thing that you can do is to stay informed on the subject. Chances are, the panic created by the media frenzy will cause its own emergency and stir everyone up to Civil unrest, rioting and a run on the stock of food and may ensue.

Therefore it is important to prepare well in advance on all of the *Things to Consider* mentioned. You do not want to be caught up in the pandemonium that will develop. *Self full-filling prophesy* is a very real aspect of human nature. If enough people believe that there is an emergency, they will most certainly create one through the anticipation.

A pandemic is an epidemic affecting a large portion of the population and over a large geographic area. If a true pandemic erupts, it will develop over a period of weeks, not overnight. Therefore, a family will have time to implement basic measures in connection with remaining in the home. Early warning will give you time to make preparations, therefore maintain an awareness of world health concerns. The internet makes such awareness much easier.

Influenza has been the most publicized pandemic agent. However, no matter which disease actually strikes, basic preparations can greatly increase the probability of survival. The isolation behavior that would be triggered by a pandemic should also remind the reader of the need to have a medical practitioner friend. Even if that practitioner could not (or would not) come to your residence to administer aid, a telephone discussion might be very helpful to those nursing the sick family member.

Your preparations should take the following into account:

- Practice good personal hygiene.
- Waste disposal becomes even more critical since improperly disposed waste and household trash can increases conditions that might breed more disease.
- Minimizing contact with the outside world until the epidemic subsides would be desirable. Efficient use of your home resources would more

important than ever. Heat, light, food and water will all be as critical as in other scenarios.

- If such a crisis arises, your understanding of how the disease is spread (direct contact, insects, airborne) will help you to take protective measures. You would need to remain as well informed as possible.
- If a pandemic outbreak occurs, state and county EMAs will have internet links as well as some locally developed information. Knowing details of the disease will help you to prepare. For a time they would be able to supply relevant current information.

You will still need to operate your household during a pandemic so all activities will need to carry on. Try to keep all sense of normalcy you can for the sake of the children. They take comfort in the routine. If a family member dies during the epidemic, it might be too dangerous to utilize the normal services of a funeral home. In that case, alternative burial arrangements would have to be made. In a true pandemic (such as the 1918 flu outbreak) many families were wiped out completely. What arrangements would parents make for the care of their children in the event both parents die?

Generic medical items to have in stock (as part of basic family medical supply stock)

- N-100 masks
- Over the counter medicines such as Ibuprofen, Acetaminophen, Aspirin, Imodium etc.
- Cough medicine
- Plastic bags (5 and 30 gallon for collecting sick room supplies)
- room humidifier
- Gator Aid or similar drinks to maintain hydration if no IV is available

Example of influenza pandemic (there have been 6 separately identified influenza pandemics during the 20th century. Note that the 1918 influenza came in three waves.

Three pandemic waves: weekly combined influenza and pneumonia mortality, United Kingdom, 1918–1919 (below)

- 1918 Influenza: the Mother of All Pandemics

Jeffery K. Taubenberger* and David M. Morens Armed Forces Institute of Pathology, Rockville, Maryland, USA; and †National Institutes of Health, Bethesda, Maryland, USA

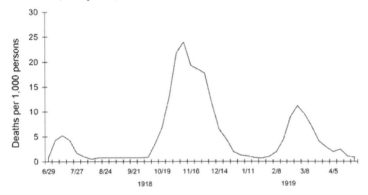

Several conditions likely to be triggered by a pandemic:

- 30% to 50% of hospital staff would be sick or afraid to come to work
- Municipal and government services would also be drastically reduced due to personnel and supply problems.
- Schools and many businesses would close, some from fear and others because of insufficient staff.
- Public health response (vaccinations) would likely be pushed into neighborhood locations instead of physician offices or hospitals.
- Many businesses would be bankrupted due to lack of produce to sell, lack of staff to do the work, or insufficient customers because they stay home.

Extended periods of Isolation may be necessary with this scenario.

⇨ *Virtually every item covered under the chapters of Things to Consider will be applicable for this scenario. Prepare for the worst and hope for the best.*

Chapter 19

EVACUATION:
THE ONLY OPTION

There are some situations where it is just not possible to stay at home. Preparations can be made in advance but during the event you will need to leave to maintain safety and security. Two scenarios stand out as being the ones were evacuation is necessary under every circumstance. In an effort to provide you with some information and to not ignore the subject all together, we have included the FEMA material for your review.

FLOOD

Mississippi County, MO, May 17, 2011 -- A roof of what once was a farm home is slowly disintegrating because of floodwaters. Mississippi County was one of several Southeast Missouri counties included in a Presidential Declaration on May 9, 2011. Steve Zumwalt/FEMA

Most homeowners who have experienced flooding will agree that it is one of the worst things that can happen to your home. I have been involved in many flood recovery situations and could wish no worse fate on anyone. Being a victim of a flood is worse than anything else including a fire, in my opinion. The contaminates enter the house with the water and deposits themselves in every nook, cranny and pore of wood in a way that only water can. It is improbable that the effects of the event will ever be completely remediated even if the structure is gutted to the framing and concrete. Mold will soon grow posing a threat to all who inhale it adding insult to injury.

You will find information provided from FEMA to follow on the subject to give some basic information dealing with the eventuality if you have no other choice. However, our advice is and will continue to be that if you are in a situation where flooding is a possibility, staying in your home and hoping to wait it out is not an option. Evacuate to higher ground and do what you have to do when you return.

Know in advance of the risks of flooding and consider an alternative location to shelter if the need arises.

The biggest question is: **Do you have a boat?**

The following are important points to remember when driving in flood conditions:[12]

- Six inches of water will reach the bottom of most passenger cars causing loss of control and possible stalling.
- A foot of water will float many vehicles.
- Two feet of rushing water can carry away most vehicles including sport utility vehicles (SUV's) and pick-ups.

After a Flood

- Listen for news reports to learn whether the community's water supply is safe to drink.
- Avoid flood waters; water may be contaminated by oil, gasoline, or raw sewage. Water may also be electrically charged from underground or downed power lines.
- Avoid moving water.
- Be aware of areas where flood waters have receded. Roads may have weakened and could collapse under the weight of a car.

---

[12] FEMA

- Stay away from downed power lines, and report them to the power company.
- Stay out of any building if it is surrounded by flood waters.
- Use extreme caution when entering buildings; there may be hidden damage, particularly in foundations.
- Service damaged septic tanks, cesspools, pits, and leaching systems as soon as possible. Damaged sewage systems are serious health hazards.
- Clean and disinfect <u>everything that got wet</u>. Mud left from floodwater can contain sewage and chemicals.

Once an automobile has been immersed in water, it is basically destroyed and will forever show the sign, (and smells) of the damage.

Flood Plain

- Formally designated flood plains are well known and defined by government and insurance companies, however other areas susceptible to localized flooding and understanding that fact is mostly a matter of common sense.
- Even if you live in a low area (not designated a flood plain) if a hard rain results in your front yard becoming a lake or if the neighborhood topography all slopes toward your front door, It is only a matter of time before enough rain falls to bring about a worst case scenario. Think about your locality and plan for what might happen.
- Consider your situation and don't continue to reside in a hazardous area.
- Heavy rain is not an instantaneous event. If you live in a canyon, valley, or low area keep the weather in mind. Remember that it doesn't have to rain directly on your area in order to flood you out. If it's raining heavily "uphill" from your location, you may get the run off.

Common flood scenarios

- In-flux of rain sets up flood conditions (combination of prolonged thunderstorms, slow moving wet weather system, or hurricane dumps excessive amount of water either directly on, or "uphill" from you. (This threat is periodic and if you are vigilant at least you can be forewarned).
- Dams pose particular danger since they may fail for a variety of reasons. Do you live below one?

149

- If you live in lowlands downstream from a dam, the threat is ever-present (you should consider moving).

Obviously, if you are facing a flood, you cannot stay where you are. If you doubt this counsel, consider the folks in New Orleans after Katrina. Breaking through the roof and being stranded there for days does not seem like an acceptable option for most people.

WILD FIRE AREA

John Haugh of Los Angeles County Fire Department's California

Practically speaking, fire is not a survivable event. There are things you can do however, to make the best of the situation when you live in a fire prone area. Walk around your house and imagine what combustible materials are nearby.

- **Decks:** A wooden deck, anchored to the house, may catch fire and act as a tender box.
    - Use fire resistant building materials and keep the area on top and underneath clear of combustible items.
    - Enclosing in with screen and covering the top with a fire resistive roofing material would be good to reduce the fire risk.
- **Yard Structures:** Pergolas, trestles and playground material close to the house will also give fire a chance to touch the building.
- **Roofing material:** Choose a class A fire rated roof material that will resist ignition.
- **Gutters:** Be sure to keep gutters clear from debris.
- **Windows:** Single pane windows can easily be shattered by the radiant heat from a fire. The open window then gives flying embers a chance to enter the house and ignite combustible materials inside. Use double pane or tempered glass to reduce the risk.
- **Fuel Storage:** If you home uses combustible materials for heating, etc, be sure they are well away from the house (at least 30'). Propane and fuel oil storage tanks present a particular hazard. Place them underground if possible. Be sure firewood is not stacked against the walls and kept at a distance.
- **Landscaping:**
    - If possible, keep surrounding bushes five feet away from the sides of the home.
    - Avoid using highly combustible mulch material such as bark, and rubber shavings, close to the house.
    - Keep dead dry material raked up and away.
    - Avoid planting under windows or near interior corners.
- **Lawn Maintenance:**
    - Keep the yard well maintained to reduce the source for fire to have fuel.
    - Keep fallen leaves cleared before they can become fuel.
    - Prune low hanging branches away from the house and away from out buildings.

- **Location consideration:**

    o   Wildfires will burn much quicker going up steep slopes and hills. If you life on the top or on the side of a hill, take this factor into consideration. You may want to create buffer zones wider than normal by keeping combustible materials farther away than otherwise recommended.

    o   If you live in a neighborhood in close proximity to each other the chance of fire spreading form one structure increases. Be sure that the siding is fire resistent; vinyl, plastic and wood would provide little resistance to a neighboring fire.

Flying embers are well known to be the primary culprit for spreading wind fires. Consider what combustible materials you have near your home that would be susceptible to this risk and do all that you can to give the fire hazard a hard time when it comes looking for you.

When it does comes time to evacuate, place a sturdy ladder in plain view against the house to assist emergency personnel in the event it is needed

   ***When considering this option, be sure
to read our companion book:***

Evacuation: A Family Guide for the 21st Century

Chapter 20

Above all, there must be:

SECURITY

New Orleans, LA 9/4/05 -- On Magazine Street, a warning to those who are thinking about looting. New Orleans is being evacuated as a result of flooding from hurricane Katrina. Photo by: Liz Roll

This section represents the authors' opinions combined with the best contemporary security wisdom available. Each individual must decide ahead of time to what degree they are willing to defend their home and family. Comprehensive security in a regional disaster may eventually become impossible. The issue of security will be approached from several different common sense aspects; namely hardening your home against intrusion and forced entry, making the premises unfriendly to intruders, and working with neighbors for mutual security.

WITHOUT SECURITY, YOU HAVE NOTHING!

If you make the decision to stay, it should be made very early. The longer this decision is delayed, the fewer options will be available. Whether you choose to evacuate or remain, move immediately to implement that decision.

Reduced to the simplest level, if you cannot assure safety and security where you are then you need to leave. Be careful not to make this decision without having all of the facts. Analyze the situation and do not overestimate your abilities. Many have decided to wait out hurricanes in their homes that did not live to tell the tale.

Establishing successful security during a crisis can be as varied as the situation itself. The decision on whether a location can be secured must be made well in advance. Law enforcement agencies may be overwhelmed and may not respond to your call for help. In some cases cell phones and land lines may be inoperable. You are on your own.

Criminals use unfortunate circumstances to take advantage of people. They have no respect for you or your property. They may attempt to get gain through petty theft, looting or robbery and assault. In most cases they are hoping for an easy target. They will avoid a site where there may be opposition, especially where lethal resistance may be encountered. Consider what you would do under those circumstances. If you are "sheltered in place" in your home, surrounded by your possessions how would you protect them?

Achieving relative security is heavily dependent on your location as much as anything else. For example, it is easier to secure a single family dwelling in the middle of a 20 acre open field than a home in a Planned Urban Development (subdivision) where there is twenty feet between the wall of one home and the next. A condominium or apartment complex presents different problems. Security is a function of minimizing known threats. There are some that are

154

known, some that are imagined and some that are not foreseen. All must be considered when outlining a security plan. A practical security plan requires thought and more thought in many dimensions, so don't expect to find all the answers in one place.

Two simple techniques could include:

- **Barriers/Barricades**: Furniture can be used as barriers. Install "Sliders" on the feet of the furniture. This makes it easy to move them against a door or window to act as barriers.
- **Safe Room:** Consider making a room in the residence to which you can retreat when security measures have failed. This will be a "hardened room": ⟹ *(See safe room construction in the Tornado Scenario.)*

It is important to remember however, that a safe room for a storm and a safe room for security purposes are two very different things. The construction of the room itself may be very similar but the location would need to be different. For example, you would most likely want to be below ground level in a storm but in an elevated position for an "over watch" security position. All of these factors should be considered when planning the location of your safe room. In all safe room scenarios, emergency supplies should be located there. Additional supplies are needed for security purposes. Tools, hammers, crowbars may be needed to escape the safe room as well as defensive supplies needed for evasion. Have a good escape plan that engages each possible scenario. In the event of a fire, you would need to leave the safe room quickly. You might not know there is a fire until it was too close and by then you would be trapped. Fire extinguishers should be strategically placed on your path to the exit. Teach the kids how to use them. They can also serve as an effective weapon.

BASIC COMMANDMENTS OF INTERIOR HOME SECURITY

- Deny entry if at all possible by hardening the premises. Intimidate threats so they look elsewhere. If entry is forced, contain the intruders into an area where they will find no cover, no hostages, and no strong points. This must be an area of your choice where the threat can be repelled or eliminated.
- If defensive action is unavoidable, eliminate the worst threat first with the hope that any followers will be discouraged and retreat in search of softer targets.
- Make prearranged specific provisions to protect spouse, children, and the

155

elderly in a secure space so you (and/or only those with defensive training) should concentrate on dealing with the threat.

- Pre-position fire suppression equipment along escape routes in case you must escape from the house due to fire. Fire demands quick escape.
- If you plan on using firearms in your security plan, take a course (or two) so you will become familiar with sound principles, legal risks and issues, and safe handling. That discussion is beyond the scope of this book and requires hands-on training.
- Don't let your own security precautions trap you in your own home.

SECURE POINTS OF ENTRY

Doors

- **Replace the screws in the door frames.** When the doors are delivered from the manufacturer to your home, they come in a thin door casing, usually ½" thick. The door is then installed into the door framing and nailed or screwed into place. The door itself is still hung to the thin frame with screws no longer than 5/8". Simply remove these screws and replace them with ones that penetrate the door casing and enter into the framing surrounding the frame with 3" screws. Usually the exterior doors are solid core. The screws into the doors themselves need not be longer than 1 ½".
- **Three points of contact:** All exterior doors should have three points of contact for the non hinged side. Simple door locks do not count as one! With a kick to the appropriate place, most doors can be opened as they rip through the thin door frame. Kick bolts in the floor, slide bolt on the top and side or chain locks should be used.
- **Door Stops/Wedges:** These are intended as a quick and effective reinforcement for the non-hinged side of the door. Driving these between the door and the frame will make it much harder to open. A string could be attached to each one making them easy to remove all at once. Drive the wedges into place using a small hammer. When the string is attached, they can be pulled out all at one time (depending on how hard you drove them into place). See the following pictures outlining the procedure.
- **Basic Door info:**
  o Solid core doors are best.
  o Hinge reinforcement (pins secured by screws are necessary or the room is easily entered)
  o Deadbolts (cheap and effective)
  o Locks (this is a place to spend money for strength)
  o Use stops and wedges

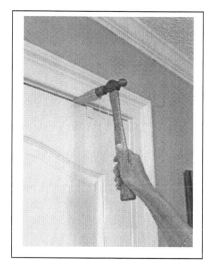 

Windows

- **Window Barrier** At least one layer of 3/4" plywood will provide a significant barrier to anyone trying to gain entry through a window. These barriers should be screwed to the outside of the window. Two layers separated by ½ of air space make a more effective barrier and will even slow a bullet considerably.
- **Window Treatments:** Curtains, blinds, tinting make observation from outside more difficult. If potential intruders cannot see inside, they are not likely to observe something that they want.
- **Close blinds and curtains** at night. Do not advertise your presence to a casual observer.
- **Cover windows** This can be done in many ways. Mattresses can be used to block windows. An easy method to store window covering plywood is to place it beneath the box springs of the bed.
  If the need arises, remove the mattress and box springs, prop the plywood in front of the window and use the slats to support the plywood against the window.

- **Mylar Film** can be installed on the inner side of the windows. It will block incoming light making it more difficult to look in.
- **Impact Glass** is expensive but effective. It is commonly used in hurricane prone areas to meet building codes.
- Upper windows that cannot be easily accessed may not need to be hardened. They should be covered to block the light but you may need this elevated point to observe your area.
- **Downstairs/basement** All windows and doors are to be fitted for barriers.
- **Thorny bushes** placed beneath all windows, these will discourage all but the most determined intruder, since forcing passage through them guarantees injury.
- **Obstructions:** Architecturally functional and aesthetically pleasing items (boulders, terraces, bamboo thickets, thorn hedges) can be used to prevent or channel vehicular traffic.

PASSIVE DETECTION TECHNIQUES

The following techniques may be useful in case you may need to leave your home and be sure no one has entered while you were away Here are a few useful techniques:

- **Mark the door:** If a room has been secured, put a strip of scotch tape between the top of the door and the frame. If the door has been opened, the seal will be broken. If you do not have any tape, put a toothpick, pencil, fishing line or coin up there. If they are not in place later then you will know what to do.
- **Mark the floor:** Spread baby powder, flour or corn starch on the floor in front of the door or window. If it has been disturbed, you will know. Also this is an effective way to determine how many people came through (the number of footprints), what type of shoe they are wearing and what size they are. The lingering powder on the shoe should indicate the direction of travel as well. This is valuable information in knowing the size and type of intruder you are facing.

FAMILY SECURITY PLAN

- **Teaching children to be aware/family buddy system:**
  - Children can be very effective in looking out for one another. A sense of this vital responsibility will help them to focus on others and not feel so helpless during a crisis. Make assignments and expect the children to carry them out. Be patient when they falter or forget, but insist that they help keep the family safe.
- **Where in the world are Mom, Dad, little Johnny, and Lisa?**
  - A crisis requires that every family member's whereabouts be accurately known.
  - This need may have to become a matter of discipline since civil authorities may not be available to help find a lost or taken family member.
  - Children and parents will need to work out a protocol whereby no one leaves the house without parents being aware and approving.
- **Family code words and alarm response.**
  - The concept of family code words is not new. Counsel together and select something that all will remember and recoqnize. Children should be instructed what to do/where to go if a parent gives the code word to them.
  - Code words can be given verbally or by a message left in a special location. Each family should pick a place where emergency messages can be left.
  - An extra set of keys for each car should be cached in a location (outside the house) known to all in case emergency transportation is necessary.

RURAL AND FARM LAND

An obvious problem with rural area security is that there are fewer people to repel intruders and longer distances between residences. Dealing with this issue is problematic. However, if this is your situation, consider some of the following issues. These residences are much more conducive to security measures, especially stand alone residences. Here is why:

- You can establish observation points where access to the property can be monitored from all directions.

159

- Defensive positions can easily be established to enforce and control access.
- Buffer zones are already in place giving the resident's time to access the threats and to take appropriate action.
- Perimeters can easily be monitored and maintained by fewer people as the line of site is less restricted.
- "Choke points" can be created to direct the aggressors to a desired location where they can be addressed. Place obstacles or take advantage of natural ones to steer the intruder to a specific area that you desire so their advance can be discouraged.
- False barricades can be provided giving the aggressor the illusion of the security or cover.
- Axle breaking rocks can be placed to restrict vehicular access.
- If you are concerned about a particular access point to your residence that will make you vulnerable to aggressors, plant Pyrocantha (thorny bushes) there. They will not go through it on foot.

Remember however, that if you live in the country there will most likely be more firearms. Those normally used for hunting and recreation can quickly be commissioned for more sinister purposes.

These are the type of thought processes that you must entertain before you consider whether to shelter in place. If you do not have security, you do not have safety and without safety you are at the mercy of your surroundings, natural and manmade.

Be aware of your environment. Where are you? Are you in an area that is prone to violence? This should have a profound impact on your choice of shelters.

WHAT IS A REAL THREAT?

You should not consider the use of deadly force as the primary means of personal security. All necessary steps should be taken to avoid it. This standard is what the law may consider when determining the presence of a legitimate threat:

Ability, Opportunity and Jeopardy (AOJ)

- **Ability:** The person had the ability to do you harm.
- **Opportunity:** The person had the opportunity to do you harm.
- **Jeopardy:** You were concerned that your safety was in jeopardy.

The operative word in connection with each of these words is "perception". If you perceived that all of these conditions your use of force was justified. This rule applies in most states but not all and can change at any time. It would be good for you to check your state law.

Let's consider what is going on in the hearts and minds of people that may be rummaging around you before, during and after and emergency occurs. You must ask yourself the question while observing an individual or individuals, what is on their mind and what are their intentions? Are they friends or do they represent a potential threat to myself or to my family.

CRIMINAL INTENT

As criminal behavior is studied, it is generally understood that violent crime is a process. Those engaged in this activity goes through various stages in caring it out.[13] These five stages are described as:

- INTENT
- INTERVIEW
- POSITIONING
- ATTACK
- REACTION

Let's go through them very briefly.

- **INTENT:**

Simply expressed, he intends to commit a crime. It is a mental decision. He has already made his mind up to do it; he is just looking for a place to carry it out. It can be preplanned or an emotional reaction to circumstances. In either event, the act of violence is an acceptable method for carrying out the crime. One

---

[13] (source: Marc MacYoung, http//nononsenceselfdefense.com/NIH.html)

easy way to determine this is to observe if a person is in the wrong place, at the wrong time and is in the wrong state of mind; if so, something is not right.

- **INTERVIEW:** This is the process of "sizing up" the target. A criminal will mostly want to get away with his crime. He will look around, maybe talk to you and feel out the situation to determine strengths and weaknesses. In this process he will decide if he can get away with it. Does he have a good escape route, is the target vulnerable and can he overpower it to get what he wants?

- **POSITIONING:**

In an assault situation, this is where he will position himself where he can attack you. The intent is to strike while you are most vulnerable, not expecting it and where you will offer the least resistance. Hence the reason for being cautious in dark hidden disserted places. These are where the techniques of surprise, cornering, trapping and surrounding are used to accomplish the criminal goal.

- **ATTACK:**

This is the application of force, usually violence used by the criminal to get what he wants. Once you have come to this stage, passive avoidance is no longer an option. Until this point, your conduct and positioning can steer the criminal away from you. Now you must react to the violence in whatever means available to you.

- **REACTION:**

OK, he has carried out the crime, now what? In many cases, the victims experience even more violent actions after the initial crime has been committed. This all depends on how the criminal feels about what he has done. Even if you have cooperated completely, he may shoot you on a whim. Remember, it does not have to make sense; these are criminals we are talking about.

When you are establishing a security scenario around your individual home or neighborhood, observe those you do not know. What are they doing, how are they behaving and do you consider them a potential threat? Use pre-established communication techniques to relay the information to those who may be able to deal with the situation in the most expeditious way.

SELF DEFENSE

Let's consider for a moment what it means to secure an area and what it means to enforce it. It is true that in time of disaster or crisis, people do crazy and ill-advised things. The city of New Orleans descended into anarchy in three days after Hurricane Katrina. There may be many people roaming around looking for something "free". That something may be yours and you may not want to give it away.

However, consider the fact that that someone rummaging through your stuff may be a person just like you, caught in an unfortunate circumstance, a victim. He is looking for something to feed his family and is just as concerned with survival as you are or, he could be a criminal looking for a place to commit a crime. Countless considerations must be made when considering the use of a weapon. Take no one's advice on what to do under certain circumstances. In most cases they have never been in the situation and do not know themselves what they would do.

If you have ever known a veteran who has served their country in times of conflict, chances are they served their country with pride. However, the things they may have had to do to defend themselves, their brothers in arms and their county is not usually a source of pride. They did what they had to do. That may be what you will have to do.

However, each and every situation is entirely different in most cases; many threatening situations can be resolved without introducing a firearm into the equation. There have been many cases, especially in years past, that police officers have served many faithful years without ever having to draw their weapons. Study every scenario out in your mind. Make a decision on what you would do and be prepared to carry out your decision

Remember that security in this scenario is defensive in nature. You are trying to protect your family and processions. Therefore the weapon you choose should be compatible to this environment. Be careful to assess the threat. It may be difficult, in fact, to determine if someone is friend of foe until they are close enough to determine their identity and/or intentions

If security has been breached in your residence, remain outside for a period of time, watch and observe. If there is movement inside you will be able to tell soon enough. Be patient and give them time to believe they are not being watched. Call for Law enforcement when available. However, if you have a good watch dog, send him in.

MOBS 101

- Mobs are 99% followers and 1% leaders.
- Mob leaders are not usually on the front lines. If they can be identified and eliminated, the mob will often disperse or move to easier targets.
- Verbal threats are ineffective. Mobs in motion are vicious, chaotic, and mindless.
- The presence of mobs presents an increased danger for travelers. If there is known mob activity then you need to stay home! Do not get on the road!
- Mobs drift where there are anticipated stores of supplies. If they believe that you have something that they need, you should take extra precautions and be prepared.

PERSONAL MOVEMENT DURING HIGH RISK SITUATIONS

(*Should* I move around?)

The decision to leave your shelter must also include the consideration on how you will return. Will the security of yourself or the shelter (and its inhabitants) be compromised if you leave? Procedures should be established prior to your departure with everyone involved, on how you will be recognized and admitted for reentry into the secured area. Consider the fact that if you are the only one on the road with transportation, you may not have it for long. Carjacking may certainly be a threat under extreme conditions. If the environment is not secure, do not travel unless it as absolutely necessary. This is especially true when civil unrest (mobs) are present. Under these circumstances it would be unwise to move about. If you are traveling by foot, between shelter locations or out looking for supplies, maintain situational awareness. Know what is going on around you. Is there anyone behind you? What are they doing? Are they looking at you?

⇨ *(Study the material on criminal behavior included in the Security section)*

Do they fit into the categories of someone who may be a threat to you? It is possible that if you look as if you are well, they may want to follow you back to your shelter. They may have determined that you have supplies there. Then you have another problem. It is OK to be paranoid! We are talking about extreme circumstances. People will do crazy things when it comes to survival.

164

SITUATIONAL AWARENESS

(Be aware of your surroundings!)

Many veterans suffer from a condition known as "hyper vigilance". These people are survivors. They can never stop looking around, wherever they go. Does someone look threatening? Is there anyone on that roof over there? Why is that car parked suspiciously on the side of the road? Do I have an escape route; where is it? Will I be able to get there?

Through training and experience they have learned to notice things the average person may not consider. They routinely scan an area before placing themselves in a vulnerable position. They have been conditioned to expect the unexpected. They are often somewhat wary of strangers and are quick to formulate a plan to take action when they sense a threat may be at hand. Have you noticed that they will rarely sit is a restaurant with their backs to the front door. They will usually walk next to the wall and always know where the exits are.

Be observant of anyone or anything you may feel to be out of place or perhaps unusual. Keep your head on a swivel and do not allow yourself to be taken by surprise. If this happens you will have little options to overcome the situation. In may be sad to consider, but this is the mindset you will have to adopt. <u>In survival situations, there is no such thing as Paranoia! Being a bit paranoid may serve you well.</u>

STEALTH

You need to be very quiet as you go about your business. Do nothing that will bring attention to yourself or to your shelter. You have people you love there. They must be protected at all costs. Every time you leave the shelter, you risk the chance to be spotted, singled out and followed, putting everyone at risk.

If you must move, have a departure route that will not expose your point of origin. Possibly, moving behind or under cover or in darkness would be good. In your return trip, be careful not to be followed; never go directly back. Stop on regular intervals. Take time to look around from a concealed place. Look at the people around you; do you recognize someone from the previous stop. If you do, emergency evasive action is needed. It is not necessary to run, just reverse course, change tactics, directions and behaviors. You may choose to lead your "friend" in the wrong direction before losing him. Do whatever it takes to keep him from finding your shelter and the loved ones inside.

If he cannot be shaken, he may have to be confronted and dealt with prior to your return. It is better that you face down the threat alone than to endanger those in the shelter. However, it is also important to remember that the loved ones in the shelter are depending on your safe return. Make sure that happens.

You may not be able to go back to the shelter for a while. This will be for as long as it takes for him to lose interest in you and go away. Of course, if you have communication (which you should), arrangements can be made to get some help. Deal with the threat. Do not give him the opportunity to exercise his criminal intentions with those you love as victims.

DEFENSIVE/SECURITY RINGS

Defensive/Security rings or Perimeters must be established. They can be improvised according to your individual circumstances. Typically, there would be three rings: outer, inner and failsafe. The distances between these rings would vary depending on the circumstance. In a rural area the rings may be 100 yards apart. In this case the rings can be identified by a large rock, tree, fence post or large bush. In an urban environment where you live in an apartment or condominium, the outer ring may be entry to the complex; the inner ring may be the entry to your particular building or floor and the failsafe would be your personal door.

Of course, improvising may need to be made; there may need to be an additional failsafe location within the residence itself. It all depends on ability to apply resistance to the rings and your ability to identify the threat and to retreat inward ring by ring. The object with the defensive rings is to make the bad guy earn his way through each one. As a result, each ring should be harder to penetrate. Obstacles or alert systems can be placed in strategic locations within the ring system to determine their rate of advance. It can be simple things that make noise when step on or through. Know in advance what you will do when each ring is reached by the aggressor and be prepared to prevent him from reaching the next interior ring.

Because of its importance, let's reset our thinking and review it again with a little different angle:

- Think of the premises in terms of defensive rings. The outer ring is to be no closer than the perimeter of your property or line of sight. Some threats may need to be addressed at that boundary

- The second ring could be the walls of your residence. Anyone who penetrates the second ring could represent an immediate and direct threat to your family's life and may be addressed accordingly.
- The third and last ring is within the walls of your residence. You may need to construct and interior safe room in case the outer defenses are breached. This area would be where a last stand would be made unless escape was possible.

LONGER TERM SECURITY CONSIDERATIONS

If the emergency situation goes on longer than expected, there may be some additional levels of security you may want to consider. Here are a few suggestions.

Organize Your Subdivision

Actually organizing your neighborhood would be a daunting task, one full of conflicting agendas and unreliable partners. It is highly unlikely that a group of people who hardly know one another would suddenly come together in an organized manner and accept a military style daily life. No family can stand completely alone in such a situation. In recent cases where regional disasters have forces entire cities to go without public services, large communities have managed to come together for a common cause. In one subdivision in particular one residence said: "you would not believe how many people came out of their houses and walked the streets meeting neighbors and asking if they can do anything to help". [14] Hopefully, this would be indicative of your situation. There will always be some that will resist organization for one reason or another; no problem, work with what you have. If nothing else, work on organizing the following areas:

Consider organizing your neighborhood along the following lines:

- **Limit Access:** (set up a checkpoint at all entrances): This could be met with some significance resistance by residents unsympathetic to your views. The Homeowners Association might be a logical place to introduce these ideas once the crisis is impending or commencing. The purpose of the checkpoint is to know who is coming and going to some degree assure that they live there. Perhaps the Homeowners Association could provide a list of residents. Officers of the law might

---

[14] Jessica Marsaw: Madison, Ala. July 2011

support this if they were not otherwise deployed. Private citizens have no legal authority to detain or restrict the movements of anyone unless they pose a direct threat. A group decision would have to be made as to whether check point personnel would attempt to actually stop persons who attempted to force entrance.

- **Communications:** Communications are necessary between checkpoints and a command center. Review the chapter on communications to determine appropriate methods. If electronic communications is not an option, set up a "runner system".

⟹ *(Study the chapter on communications and consider possible variations to fit your situation).*

- **Create Buffer zones**: A buffer zone is a strip of real-estate where access can be monitored and/or controlled. Residential developments are not usually built with perimeters or buffer zones (except green space which presents several problems).
- **Observation positions**: Set up as many positions as necessary so approaches to the area can be monitored. Communications must be fashioned so observations can be passed between remote positions and a central location. This flow of information is necessary for leadership to compose a realistic picture of area activity.
- **Medical Support:** Identify and attempt to recruit doctors, nurses, EMTs or other medically trained people. If you find persons willing to contribute some medical expertise, attempt to establish a permanent location where examination and/or treatment can be carried out. In most cases, they will be willing to offer any assistance needed. Possibly, their residence can be the make shift first aid station. Of course, it is important to understand that particularly in times of disaster; these folks will be hard to come by. They will most likely be needed to assist in the larger need and will working in the hospital or clinics.
- **A support team** to help one another if the need arises: During times of disaster, the best and worst of peoples character is displayed. Once you have developed a team for mutual support, you will probably be astonished as to the level of compassion and selflessness for each other you will see. Try to create a group to travel among the community to determine specific needs and to coordinate available resources to assist. If security is a concern, the travel/movement aspect should be carried out by those best able to deal with any situation that may arise.

168

CASE STUDY

Consider the different areas of concern mentioned for providing a limited amount of security for your neighborhood. In the following page you will find an image of a typical American suburban neighborhood with several hundred homes. It will be unlikely that you will obtain a mutual understanding with a large number of people in your development regarding the establishment of security measures. However, if you can get a few and place them in strategic locations, you can provide the most essential security services.

Let's consider these issues we discussed earlier in this case study one at a time using the example shown.

1. **Limit Access:** There are five vehicular access points to the subdivision as indicated. The front of the homes faces the interior streets. Because the yards are fenced, all vehicles would gain access by the main entrances indicated. These points could be monitored or restricted as needed. You may consider posting a sign on the side of the road before each entrance to the development. The message itself may be a sufficient deterrent to turn a would be bad guy away.

    YOU ARE ENTERING A CONTROLED AREA BE PREPARED TO SHOW ID

2. **Communications:** Radio communication could be established at each of the access checkpoints as well as the observation points, command center (if applicable) and any medical facilities located within the development.

3. **Buffer Zones:** In this particular case, there are natural buffer zones already in place. The main street itself running along the perimeter of the development serves as one although it is thin and active. The buffer zone would be the narrow strip of land between the side of the road the the fence line of the residences' yard. Along the north, there is a creek/wooded area just behind the clubhouse. This is a wider area and easier to spot intruders.

Clubhouse

(Image: Google Earth)

Vehicular Access Points:

4. **Observation Positions**: In this case study, the streets are mostly long and straight. An observation post can be established on either end of the street that would allow a view of the street at its full length. An elevated position could easily be established with an extension latter and a comfortable perch on a roof top. Of course, the more observers the better. Place them on corners where they can observe multiple areas at once. Give each of them communications equipment and binoculars. These will become the "watchmen on the tower" and a most critical position in the security scenario. The clubhouse is located in a strategic point for observation. An observer located on the roof of this facility will be able to view a large area including buffer zones to the north.

5. **Medical Support**:   As mentioned earlier, it is hopeful that someone with medical training can be located within your group. Hopefully, you will be able to locate this facility safely within the interior of the development where maximum security can be provided.

6. **Support team:** There will be a great need for these types of people. They should be utilized to roam between stations to provide assistance as needed and to determine their individual needs. Food, Hydration and friendly support will be in great demand.

In the "worse case" scenario, you may need to consider the possibility that your subdivision will never be secure. Unless you are an extraordinary group, it will be difficult if not impossible to get so many like minded people on the same page as you. They will want to come and go as they please and be accountable to no one and there will be nothing you can do about it. Chances are that many will scatter to the wind as they go to other locations with friends and family leaving many homes vacant leaving you to deal with the situation there. Adjust, adapt and improvise the best you can; that is all that you can do.

Take an inventory of those willing to help out and agree to assist in the cause. Ask those not willing to help to only not interfere.

Let's make some assumptions regarding this group.

Subdivision *Alpha:* (300 homes)

Of the total number of people: 1050, (3.5/ home)

Adults over 30 years old:	40%
Adults between 21 and 30 years old:	24%
Youth between 16 and 21 years old:	18%
Youth less than 16 years old:	18%
	100%

Necessary Responsibilities	# of Shifts	# of Teams	# staff needed each	total
A. Coordinating Team	3	1	10	30
B. Security	3	1	2	6
o Checkpoints	3	5	4	6
o SOP[15]	3	8	1	24
o Roving Patrol	4	3	2	24
o Response Team	3	3	3	18
C. Medical	4	1	4	16
D. Food/Supplies	1	50	50	50
E. Communications				
o Local [16]	3	1	15	45
o Outside Comm. 1	5	1	1	5
F. School				
o Teaching Children	1	1	8	8
o Teach Adult Skills	1	1	10	10
o Other	1	1	5	5

Total Assigned: 247

G. Those not participating[17]   (77%)   **803**

Overall Total   1050

Let's reviews each responsibility by narrative:

A. Coordinating team: There will need to be a group of individuals assigned to receive all incoming communications and to coordinate response as needed. It would include but not limited to security. Depending on the circumstances and the level of activity needing attention it could be staffed between six to twelve people.

B. Security:

o **Checkpoints**: In this particular scenario, there are five entry points to the subdivision. There would be three shifts with four people at each checkpoint.

o

---

[15] SOP: Stationary Observation Posts as needed to do the job (we assume 8)

[16] See chapter on communications: FRS/GMRS/CB/HAM

[17] Includes small children, older, infirmed residents and the unwilling.

- ○ **SOP:** Stationary Observation Points would be where people would be positioned in strategic positions throughout the development to see all that is happening. They would have communications with the Base coordinator to report any item needing attention.
- ○ **Roving Patrol:** Three teams of two people on three shifts would roam the facility by foot or any other means necessary. Their responsibility would be to observe the integrity of the perimeters and the condition of the individual facilities. They would check in on those needing continued assistance and communicate the need to the base coordinator so he can coordinate assistance.
- ○ **Response Team:** This would be a group of three trained individuals who would be on "standby" ready to respond to a specific need should they be directed by the base coordinator. It could be to respond to a reported breach in security at the checkpoint or on the perimeters.

C. **Medical**: Hopefully there will be someone in the development with medical training that would volunteer to be of assistance when needed. We would suggest four shifts of four people each.

D. **Food/Supplies** the degree of preparedness will greatly vary within the community. We are proposing that a large group be assembled to determine the needs of the individuals within the development. Specific needs should be determined and efforts made to meet the need. Of course, if the mentality of "every man for himself" has prevailed then ignore this suggestion.

E. **Communications**: Communications is most critical in every aspect of this endeavor. Study the chapter on communications to determine how best to meet this need. There will need to be significant local comm. between the various responsibilities within the shifts and to the base coordinator. (Local) there will also need to be someone monitoring the "outside world" for news and information that may affect the community at large.

F. **School:** It is understood that this consideration would only come into play in a worst case scenario and that it reaches beyond the scope and intent of this material. However, if the emergency surpasses a few weeks it would be beneficial in all respects to occupy the children and adults with something to engage their time in a productive way.

One of the purposes of this exercise is to illustrate how large the numbers are but also, with only 23% of the total participating in the plan, you could create an effective working team.

Here are a few additional things for you to consider:

- Working with like minded (and not so like minded) volunteers
  - Organizing a neighborhood requires that you patiently sift through neighbors to see if they are willing to do anything at all, and if so are they willing to work together.
  - If they are willing to work together, proposing a beginning structure will at least give you somewhere to start. As you open this discussion you will identify like minded persons with whom you have a chance of working.
  - Some neighbors will NEVER see things as you do. You have no authority to compel their compliance, nor can you demand their cooperation.
  - Be patient, respectful and honest.

- A new "normal" everyday life – reestablishing daily life and charting your new direction

(Previous photo) Apalachicola, Fla., July 20, 2005 -- Warning sign to looters at a damaged business. The owners placed the damaged goods outside in front of the business. Damage to businesses due to storm surge following Hurricane Dennis. FEMA photo/Andrea Booher

CONCLUSION

The decision to stay at home during an emergency should be made after careful consideration to the specifics of the emergency and the family situation. It may be the best thing to do, or it may prove to be fatal. However, consider this fact for a moment: if you did not think it was an important issue, why are you reading this?

Because you are here now and considering making these preparations, the little "voice" inside you has prompted you to get ready, maybe just a little bit. No one knows your capabilities and your family needs better than you do. Study the possible scenarios carefully. Consider how they could impact you and make a decision based on solid information.

Be careful not to overestimate your ability to overcome some of these emergencies. However and by the same token, do not underestimate you ability to overcome these emergencies if you are properly prepared. What will contribute most to success is prior planning.

Consider the most likely emergency you will face. Begin preparations now to deal with that situation. Take it one step at a time. If you live in a tornado prone area, begin now to build a safe room. Lay it out in your mind, sit down with your family and begin the process. Then, work on the supplies you will need to have in the safe room.

Work on food, water and communications in order of priority. Talk to your neighbors about what your plans are on security. Consider creating a neighborhood or family group and work through the issues together. When things get stressful, people have a tendency to change. Be sure that you know them well. Have only people you can trust on the team.

Pool your resources for food, water equipment that will be needed and have them staged in the shelter or in a location where they can quickly and easily be transported there.

Consider the scenarios carefully and create a plan on what you would do under certain circumstances. Communicate this plan to your family and anyone else that it would include. Be sure that you stay in touch often to assure that communication channels are current. Keep up with changes in the environment that would have an effect on the plan. Adjust and adapt the plan as needed.

Use your head. Make good judgments. Trust yourself. Maintain situational awareness and be a good steward of the trust others have place in you. Do not put your family's safety on the line by trying to shelter through something you should not. If you live on the beach and a category 5 storm is bearing down on you: LEAVE. If you are in a home that will be flooded: leave. There are things you can do and things you should not do. You cannot stay in your home if the surrounding forest is on fire.

However, with those qualifications being made, there are many emergency situations you can make it through just fine. It will bring you much comfort to know that you are prepared. Dedicate yourself *to making this thing work*.

If you do this you will be an example to those around you. They will take courage in your example. Help them all that you can. You will both benefit in the end.

Simply said: DO IT! Get ready; make the preparations you need to so that if (or when) the time comes, you will be ready to go. Mobilize your resources and do not try to do it all by yourself. Ask friends who share your concerns to assist in the effort.

Good Luck!

WORKSHEETS
&
REFERENCE MATERIAL

Action checklist:

1) Assess the most likely emergencies you will face.

Possible Scenarios	Level of Concern (1-5)
1. Tornado	
2. Hurricane	
3. Earthquake	
4. Winter Storm	
5. Nuclear	
6. Volcano	
7. Civil Unrest	
8. Flood	
9. Wildfire	
10. Pandemic	

2) Study: Things to Consider

Things to Consider	Level of Concern (1-5)
1. Food/ water	
2. Sanitation	
3. Children	
4. Electrical	
5. Medical	
6. Where to shelter	
7. Transportation/Movement	
8. Security	
9. Communications	
10. Insurance	

3) Create your action plan and determine a completion date –
discuss with all family members as you make progress.

	Priority	Action Plan	By when
	1. Food/ water		
	2. Sanitation		
	3. Children		
	4. Electrical		
	5. Medical		
	6. Where to shelter		
	7. Transportation/ Movement		
	8. Security		
	9. Communications		
	10. Insurance		

4) Evacuation plan (just in case): **see separate form.**

5) Distribute the written plan to all involved.

6) Schedule dates, review and revise as needed.

7) Share your thoughts and ideas with others who are
interested.

Evacuation Plan

(Just in case)

Name

_____

How will we know the plan has been activated? (In case you are separated)

_____

How will the activation of the plan be communicated?

_____

What is the **level of Preparation?** _____

Where are the **Rally Points?**

Primary (1):

_____

Secondary
(2):_____

Emergency/Fail safe (3): _____

What is the **departure route?**

_____

_____

Alternate Route:

_____

_____

Go Bags
Which bag is assigned to whom?

Person	Which Bag

What is your **ultimate destination?**
Primary (D1) _____
Secondary (D2): _____
Emergency/Fail safe: _____

Method of Communications?

	Person	How
Mom/Dad		
Kids		
Extended Family		
Possible Host		

Distribute copies to all family members.

You may use this template to point you in the right direction.
Adjust and adapt as needed.

Go-Bag (72 hours) list (to have in shelter or for evacuation)

Water: pack at least one gallon of water. You will need one gallon each day to avoid debilitating dehydration.

Food: This food is for emergency only.

Clothing: Change into traveling clothes before beginning evacuation if possible, comfortable shoes (sneakers, hikers), already broken in! Two changes of underwear rip stop pants, poncho, three changes of socks, two t-shirts, down or poly filled jacket with waterproof breathable shell, floppy hat with brim, composite (warm) gloves.

Fire starters: Carry all of the following: matches, flint and steel, and a butane lighter.

Flashlight and spare batteries: LED or wind up flash lights

First aid kit: Carry only a small basic first aid package.

Toilet paper: remove the cardboard tube and flatten the roll to save space. Store in a zip lock freezer bag.

Lip balm: You will become dehydrated, and this will help.

Sun screen: SPF 30, it must be used to be effective.

Fishing-line: "just in case"

Parachute cord: 50 ft (15 m).

Duct tape: Store in zip lock bag.

Personal items: Soap, toothbrush, toothpaste, and floss. Personal hygiene (women's hygiene and/or baby care) is essential for survival.

Garbage bags: 2 (30 gal), extra zip lock or poncho.

Sleeping bag: or cold weather pants

Compass and topographical map: of every county you'll traverse on the way to your primary or alternate destination.

Pepper spray or other defensive items: use your own best judgment, and remain within legal bounds

Pencil and paper. To leave notes if necessary

Multi-tool and sheath knife

MRE at least one so you don't have to cook one meal **Emergency Whistle** for signaling

Other convenience items: tent (dome type is easy to set up in a small area, and may not require lines and tent pegs) one small aluminum pot with lid, utensils, alcohol stove, GPS/compass and GMRS/FRS (2 meter HAM is best) radio transceiver, 8×10 tarp, compact survival plant reference guide, survival knife, military folding entrenching tool or small shovel

Cash: Small bills

THREE MONTH FOOD SUPPLY SHOULD INCLUDE:

Baking ingredients

Baking chips (butterscotch, milk
    chocolate, semisweet, white, etc.
Baking powder
Baking soda
Coca
Coconut
Corn Meal
Corn syrup
Cornstarch
Cream of tartar
Extracts (almond, maple, mint,
    vanilla)
Flour (all purpose, bread, etc)
Food Coloring
Gelatin (flavored, plain)
Honey
Marshmallows
Milk (evaporated, sweetened
    Condensed)
Molasses
Nonstick cooking spray
Nuts (almonds, peanuts, pecans
    Walnuts)
Oil (olive, vegetable)
Pie filling
Salt and pepper
Shortening
Spices (cinnamon, ginger, nutmeg,
    etc)
Sugar (brown, confectioners',
    Granulated)
Tapioca (quick-cooking)
Yeast

Baking Mixes

Biscuit
Brownie
Cake
Corn bread
Frosting (canned)
Muffin
Pancake
Pudding (instant)
Quick bread

Canned or bottled foods

Applesauce
Beans (black, great northern,
    kidney, pinto, etc.)
Broth (beef, chicken)
Fruits (fruit cocktail, mandarin
    oranges, peaches, pears,
    pineapple, etc.)
Green Chilies
Jam and Jelly
Ketchup
Meats (beef, chicken, ham, etc)
Mushrooms
Olives
Peanut butter
Prepared entrees (chili, ravioli,
    Spaghetti, soups, stews, etc.)
Salsa
Sauces (alfredo, cheese, picante,
    spaghetti, etc.)
Soups, condenced (chicken,
    mushroom, celery, etc.)
Tomatoes (diced, paste, sauce,
    stewed)
Tuna
    Vegetables (corn, beans, peas)

Dried Fruits and Veggies

Apples
Apricots
Carrots
Celery
Cranberries
Dates
Onions
Garlic
Peppers (bell, hot, etc.)
Prunes
Raisins
Tomatoes

Seasonings

Bouillon granules (beef, chicken)
 Browning and seasoning sauce
Hot pepper sauce
Onion soup mix
 Seasoned salt
Soy sauce
Taco seasoning
Vinegar (balsamic, cider)
Worcestershire sauce

Starches

Bread (pita, sandwich)
Bread crumbs, dry
Crackers (graham, soda, etc)
Croutons
Noodle mixes
Pasta (noodles, macaroni, penne,
  spaghetti, etc.)
Rice (instant)
Rice mixes
Stuffing mix

Storage (long term)

Dried beans (black, kidney, navy,
  Pinto)
Nonfat dry milk powder
Oats (regular, instant)
Potato (flakes, pearls)
Rice (instant, long grain, etc)
Wheat (red or white)
Egg powder

FAMILY ID CARD

The attitude of "prepare for the worst hope for the best" would be a good attitude to have. Things may not go as planned.
Make copies of this form and put in zip lock bags or waterproof sheet protector on each person bag in the unfortunate event you become separated. This is especially important for the kids.

Photograph
Date of photograph: _____

Name
_____

Last Address:

Blood type _____ allergies _____
Special medical needs _____
Please contact my parents

Primary Rally point
_____
_____
_____
Names_____

Secondary Rally Point

_____

_____

Emergency Rally Point:

_____

PRIMARY TELEPHONE CONTACT NUMBERS

HOME_____

CELL _____

NEAREST RELATIVES

1) NAME _____

ADDRESS _____

PHONE NUMBERS _____

2) NAME _____

ADDRESS _____

PHONE NUMBERS _____

ALTERNATE CONTACTS

1) Name _____

STREET_____

CITY_____

STATE_____

HOME PHONE_____

CELL _____

2) Name _____

STREET_____

CITY _____

STATE _____

HOME PHONE_____

CELL_____

Good things to have around the shelter

Tools and Supplies
* Mess kits, or paper cups, plates, and plastic utensils
* Emergency preparedness manual
* Battery-operated radio and extra batteries
* Flashlight and extra batteries
* Cash or traveler's checks, change
* Non-electric can opener, utility knife
* Fire extinguisher: small canister ABC type
* Tube tent or camping/backpack tent
* Pliers
* Tape
* Compass
* Matches in a waterproof container
* Aluminum foil
* Plastic storage containers
* Signal flare
* Paper, pencil
* Needles, thread
* Medicine dropper
* Shut-off wrench, to turn off household gas and water
* Whistle
* Plastic sheeting
* Map of the area (for locating shelters)

Sanitation
 *Toilet paper, "towelettes"
* Soap, liquid detergent
* Feminine supplies
* Personal hygiene items
* Plastic garbage bags, ties (for personal sanitation uses)
* Plastic bucket with tight lid
* Disinfectant
* Household chlorine bleach

Clothing and Bedding
*Include at least one complete change of clothing and footwear per person.
* Sturdy shoes or work boots
* Rain gear*
* Blankets or sleeping bags
* Hat and gloves

* Thermal underwear
* Sunglasses

Special Items
* Remember family members with special requirements, such as infants and elderly or disabled persons

For Baby
* Formula
* Diapers
* Bottles
* Powdered milk
* Medications

For Adults
* Heart and high blood pressure medication
* Insulin
* Prescription drugs
* Denture needs
* Contact lenses and supplies
* Extra eye glasses

Entertainment
* Games and books

Important Family Documents
* Keep these records in a waterproof, portable container:
    * Will, insurance policies, contracts deeds, stocks and bonds
    * Passports, social security cards, immunization records
    * Bank account numbers
    * Credit card account numbers and companies
    * Inventory of valuable household goods, important telephone numbers
    * Family records (birth, marriage, death certificates)
    * Store your kit in a convenient place known to all family members
    * Keep a smaller version of the supplies kit in the trunk of your car.
    * Keep items in airtight plastic bags.
    * Change your stored water supply every six months so it stays fresh.
    * Replace your stored food every six months. Re-think your kit and family needs at least once a year.
    * Replace batteries, update clothes, etc.
    * Ask your physician or pharmacist about storing prescription medications.

189

List of 100 things that might quickly become scarce during a crisis

1. Generators (Good ones cost dearly. Gas storage, risky, noisy)
2. Water Filters/Purifiers
3. Portable Toilets
4. Seasoned Firewood. Wood takes about 6 – 12 months to dry for home use.
5. Lamp Oil, Wicks, Lamps (First Choice: Buy CLEAR oil. If scarce, stockpile ANY!)
6. Coleman Fuel. Impossible to stockpile too much.
7. Guns, Ammunition, Pepper Spray, Knives, Clubs, Bats & Slingshots. (for display purposes)
8. Hand-can openers, & hand egg beaters, whisks.
9. Honey/Syrups/white, brown sugar
10. Rice – Beans – Wheat
11. Vegetable Oil (for cooking) Without it food burns/must be boiled etc.,)
12. Charcoal, Lighter Fluid (Will become scarce suddenly)
13. Water Containers (Urgent Item to obtain.) Any size. Small: HARD CLEAR PLASTIC ONLY – (Note: food grade if for drinking).
14. Mini Heater head (Propane) (Without this item, propane won't heat a room.)
15. Grain Grinder (Non-electric)
16. Propane Cylinders (Urgent: Definite shortages will occur).
17. Survival Guide Book.
18. Mantles: Aladdin, Coleman, etc. (Without this item, longer-term lighting is difficult.)
19. Baby Supplies: Diapers/formula. Ointments/aspirin, etc.
20. Washboards, Mop Bucket w/wringer (for Laundry)
21. Cook stoves (Propane, Coleman & Kerosene)
22. Vitamins
23. Propane Cylinder Handle-Holder (Urgent: Small canister use is dangerous without this item)
24. Feminine Hygiene/Hair care/Skin products.
25. Thermal underwear (Tops & Bottoms)
26. Bow saws, axes and hatchets, Wedges (also, honing oil)
27. Aluminum Foil Reg. & Heavy Duty (Great Cooking and Barter Item)
28. Gasoline Containers (Plastic & Metal)
29. Garbage Bags (Impossible To Have Too Many).
30. Toilet Paper, Kleenex, Paper Towels
31. Milk – Powdered & Condensed (Shake Liquid every 3 to 4 months)
32. Garden Seeds (Non-Hybrid) (A MUST)
33. Clothes pins/line/hangers (A MUST)
34. Coleman's Pump Repair Kit

35. Tuna Fish (in oil)
36. Fire Extinguishers (or large box of Baking Soda in every room)
37. First aid kits
38. Batteries (all sizes…buy furthest-out from Expiration Dates)
39. Garlic, spices & vinegar, baking supplies
40. Big Dogs (and plenty of dog food)
41. Flour, yeast & salt
42. Matches. {"Strike Anywhere" preferred.) Boxed, wooden matches will go first
43. Writing paper/pads/pencils, solar calculators
44. Insulated ice chests (good for keeping items from freezing in wintertime.)
45. Work boots, belts, Levis & durable shirts
46. Flashlights/LIGHTSTICKS & torches, "No. 76 Dietz" Lanterns
47. Journals, Diaries & Scrapbooks (jot down ideas, feelings, experience; Historic Times)
48. Garbage cans Plastic (great for storage, water, transporting – if with wheels)
49. Shampoo, Toothbrush/paste, Mouthwash/floss, nail clippers, etc
50. Cast iron cookware (sturdy, efficient)
51. Fishing supplies/tools
52. Mosquito coils/repellent sprays/creams
53. Duct Tape
54. Tarps/stakes/twine/nails/rope/spikes
55. Candles
56. Laundry Detergent (liquid)
57. Backpacks, Duffel Bags
58. Garden tools & supplies
59. Scissors, fabrics & sewing supplies
60. Canned Fruits, Veggies, Soups, stews, etc.
61. Bleach (plain, **NOT** scented: 4 to 6% sodium hypochlorite)
62. Canning supplies, (Jars/lids/wax)
63. Knives & Sharpening tools: files, stones, steel
64. Bicycles…Tires/tubes/pumps/chains, etc
65. Sleeping Bags & blankets/pillows/mats
66. Carbon Monoxide Alarm (battery powered)
67. Board Games, Cards, Dice
68. D-con Rat poison, MOUSE PRUFE II, Roach Killer
69. Mousetraps, Ant traps & cockroach magnets
70. Paper plates/cups/utensils (stock up, folks)
71. Baby wipes, oils, waterless & Antibacterial soap (saves a lot of water)
72. Rain gear, rubberized boots, etc.
73. Shaving supplies (razors & creams, talc, after shave)
74. Hand pumps & siphons (for water and for fuels)
75. Soy sauce, vinegar, bullions/gravy/soup base

76. Reading glasses
77. Chocolate/Cocoa/Tang/Punch (water enhancers)
78. "Survival-in-a-Can"
79. Woolen clothing, scarves/ear-muffs/mittens
80. Boy Scout Handbook, / also Leaders Catalog
81. Roll-on Window Insulation Kit (MANCO)
82. Graham crackers, saltines, pretzels, Trail mix/Jerky
83. Popcorn, Peanut Butter, Nuts
84. Socks, Underwear, T-shirts, etc. (extras)
85. Lumber (all types)
86. Wagons & carts (for transport to and from)
87. Cots & Inflatable mattres'
88. Gloves: Work/warming/gardening, etc.
89. Lantern Hangers
90. Screen Patches, glue, nails, screws, nuts & bolts
91. Teas
92. Coffee
93. Cigarettes
94. Wine/Liquors (for bribes, medicinal, etc,)
95. Paraffin wax
96. Glue, nails, nuts, bolts, screws, etc.
97. Chewing gum/candies
98. Atomizers (for cooling/bathing)
99. Hats & cotton neckerchiefs
100. Goats/chickens

BACKFEED GENERATOR PROCEDURE

Before starting

1. The generator is fueled, oil checked, properly positioned so exhaust is not discharging into an occupied dwelling
2. Position fuel containers 50 feet away, and verify that they are properly closed
3. Verify which individual breakers control which appliances you wish to activate
4. Turn house main panel breaker switch **off**, place a piece of duct tape over the main switch so no one can throw it to the on position without first removing the tape.
5. Warn all members of the household to avoid the vicinity of generator **and** the receptacle where power is being fed in
6. Turn off **all** individual circuit breakers
7. Connect one end of the pigtail to the generator, connect the other end to the house receptacle you will use to bring power into the house
8. Start the generator and allow it to achieve a smooth idle
9. One at a time, throw individual breakers to the on position until chosen appliances are receiving power.
10. **NOTE:** after throwing each breaker to the on position, pause for half a minute verify that the generator is running smoothly and not slowing down. Under load the generator engine should speed up and sound like it is working harder

Shut down

1. Close each individual breaker until all are shut down
2. Shut down generator, and wait until it stops completely
3. Disconnect the pigtail from both the input receptacle and the generator
4. Undertake generator fueling and maintenance as required
5. Be sure the generator is secured so it cannot easily be stolen

U.S. EMERGENCY AGENCY INFORMATION LINKS

NOTE: these links may be changed without notice at any time by the respective states

Alabama http://ema.alabama.gov/CountyEMA/Index.cfm
Alaksa http://www.ak-prepared.com/
Arizona http://www.dem.azdema.gov/
Arkansas http://www.adem.arkansas.gov/
California http://www.oes.ca.gov/
Colorado http://www.dola.state.co.us/dem/index.html
Connecticut http://www.ct.gov/demhs/site/default.asp
Delaware http://dema.delaware.gov/
Florida http://www.floridadisaster.org/
Georgia http://www.gema.ga.gov/
Hawaii http://www.honolulu.gov/dem/
Idaho http://www.bhs.idaho.gov/
Illinois http://www.state.il.us/iema/index.asp
Indiana http://www.in.gov/dhs/
Iowa http://www.iowahomelandsecurity.org/
Kansas http://www.kansas.gov/kdem/
Kentucky http://kyem.ky.gov/
 Louisiana http://gohsep.la.gov/default.aspx
Maine http://www.state.me.us/mema/
Maryland http://www.mema.state.md.us/MEMA/index.jsp
Massachusetts http://www.mass.gov/?pageID=eopshomepage
      &L=1&L0=Home&sid=Eeops
Michigan http://www.michigan.gov/msp/0,1607,7-123- 1593_3507---,00.html
Minnesota http://www.hsem.state.mn.us/
Mississippi http://www.msema.org/
Missouri http://sema.dps.mo.gov/
Montana http://www.dphhs.mt.gov/PHSD/PHEP-training
      /phep-training-emi.shtml
Nebraska http://www.getting-ready.com/preparedness/
      nebraskaemergencymanagementagencynema.html
Nevada http://www.dem.state.nv.us/
New Hampshire http://www.nh.gov/safety/divisions/hsem/
New Jersey http://www.state.nj.us/njoem/

New Mexico http://www.nmdhsem.org/default.asp?
New York http://www.semo.state.ny.us/
North Carolina http://www.nccrimecontrol.org

North Dakota http://www.nd.gov/des/
Ohio http://ema.ohio.gov/
Oklahoma http://www.ok.gov/oem/
Oregon http://www.oregon.gov/OMD/OEM/
Pennsylvania http://www.pema.state.pa.us/portal/
     server.pt/community/pema_home/4463
Rhode Island http://www.riema.ri.gov/
South Carolina http://www.scemd.org/
South Dakota http://dps.sd.gov/emergency
     _services/emergency_management/default.aspx
Tennessee http://www.tnema.org/
Texas http://www.txdps.state.tx.us/dem/
Utah http://publicsafety.utah.gov/index.html
Vermont http://www.dps.state.vt.us/vem/
Virginia http://www.vdem.state.va.us/
West Virginia http://www.wvdhsem.gov/
Wisconsin http://emergencymanagement.wi.gov/
Wyoming http://wyohomelandsecurity.state.wy.us/main.aspx
FEMA http://www.fema.gov/
Yellowstone Caldera Volcano Observatory http://volcanoes.usgs.gov/yvo/
Volcano Precautions
     http://www.volcanolive.com/news.html (very informative volcano web
     site)

     http://volcanoes.usgs.gov/ (volcano hazards program page)

     http://avo.alaska.edu/ (Alaska Redoubt volcano information page)
     http://volcanoes.usgs.gov/ash/todo.html (to do lists)

11586729R00112

Made in the USA
Charleston, SC
07 March 2012